I0825323

WOMEN OF KUWAIT

Maha Alasaker & Nada Faris

Daylight

Cofounders: Taj Forer and Michael Itkoff
Creative Director: Ursula Damm

ISBN 978-1-942084-66-2

Printed by Artron, China

Daylight Books
E-mail: info@daylightbooks.org
Web: www.daylightbooks.org

This is for you, Mama Shaikah and Aunt Fozia.
I couldn't have done this without your love and support.

FOREWORD

—Lulual Sabah

In understanding the value of art as a means of expression, particularly as a means to express internal pain, Maha Alasaker gives a voice to those who are often voiceless.

As a young country, gaining its independence in 1961, Kuwait aspires to be a nation made up of equal citizens. Article 29 of the Kuwaiti constitution states, "All people are equal in human dignity and in public rights and duties before the law, without distinction as to gender, origin, language or religion." However, Kuwait has undeniably maintained a legal framework that discriminates against women, and in doing so violates the integrity of the constitution.

For example, up until 2005, the election law of 1962 stipulated that voters could only be male. To date there are still many discrepancies in matters pertaining to marriage, divorce, guardianship, and citizenship that put women at a disadvantage. Yet it would be a mistake to perceive Kuwaiti women solely as an oppressed mass. In her series *Women of Kuwait*, Alasaker challenges this one-dimensional representation of Kuwaiti women.

In this series, Alasaker photographs women of various ages and social backgrounds within their most intimate space—their bedroom. Each photograph shows a woman dressed in her own choice of clothing within her own personal surroundings, shedding light on each woman's taste and hobbies. This is at the opposite end of the spectrum from a formal portrait, wherein a woman is captured in full makeup and formal attire, or in places frequented by guests, such as the living room, or in public. By featuring Kuwaiti women in the place where they sleep, dream, and experience their most guarded thoughts and feelings, Alasaker offers a glimpse into their private, more authentic selves, capturing her subjects in a less performance- and image-based setting. The broad range of her subjects encompasses a chef, a senior executive, a financial researcher, an economist, a stylist and a veterinarian, showcasing the wide array of Kuwaiti women's professional ambitions. From single working mothers to married entrepreneurs, the women are not pigeonholed by their nationality, gender, or marital status. Transcending these categories, Alasaker portrays the uniqueness of each individual and their specific thoughts on the status of women in Kuwait. This series is both an acknowledgment and a celebration of their individuality and dynamic personalities, shedding the masks that women are socialized to wear within society.

An underlying theme in Alasaker's work is the status of women and the conflicting emotions and feelings that arise from being subjected to a set of rules, both spoken and unspoken, that females are expected to adhere to. In an earlier series, titled *Belonging*, she addressed the double lives that many women have in Kuwait, a mechanism to avoid scrutiny and to save one's own sanity. In another series—created specifically for an NGO and titled *Abolish 153*, which aims to abolish laws in Kuwait that are violent and discriminatory toward women—Alasaker depicts the female form, a flower (lily), and a wet white veil. The images were taken with a 35mm camera. The negatives were scanned and retouched digitally, then printed in a small format and presented in pairs, so that the viewer had to come close to the images to decipher their meaning. Those works spoke of beauty, fragility, propriety, and the colonization of women's bodies.

Alasaker's desire to challenge the limited perspective of Arab women in general and Kuwaiti women in particular emanates from her own journey in manifesting her potential as an artist. Alasaker is based in New York, where she produces commercial photography to support herself and fine art photography as her passion. It is with sheer determination that Alasker pursued her love for photography, then used this medium to highlight the plight of women in her own country, focusing on their strengths and complexity. She broke through many boundaries in her creative process, and in doing so serves as an inspiration to many women, especially those from conservative backgrounds. Alasaker presents work that is socially relevant, highlighting divisive topics such as the marginalized role of women in Kuwaiti society and the Arab world as a whole. She understands how culture shapes individuals and the extent to which restrictions and constraints put pressure on the expression of one's individuality, especially in a society where women are often judged and criticized for nonconformity. Alasaker dared to be different, and therefore knows that inner strength is needed to pursue one's ambitions and, most important, to be true to one's authentic self.

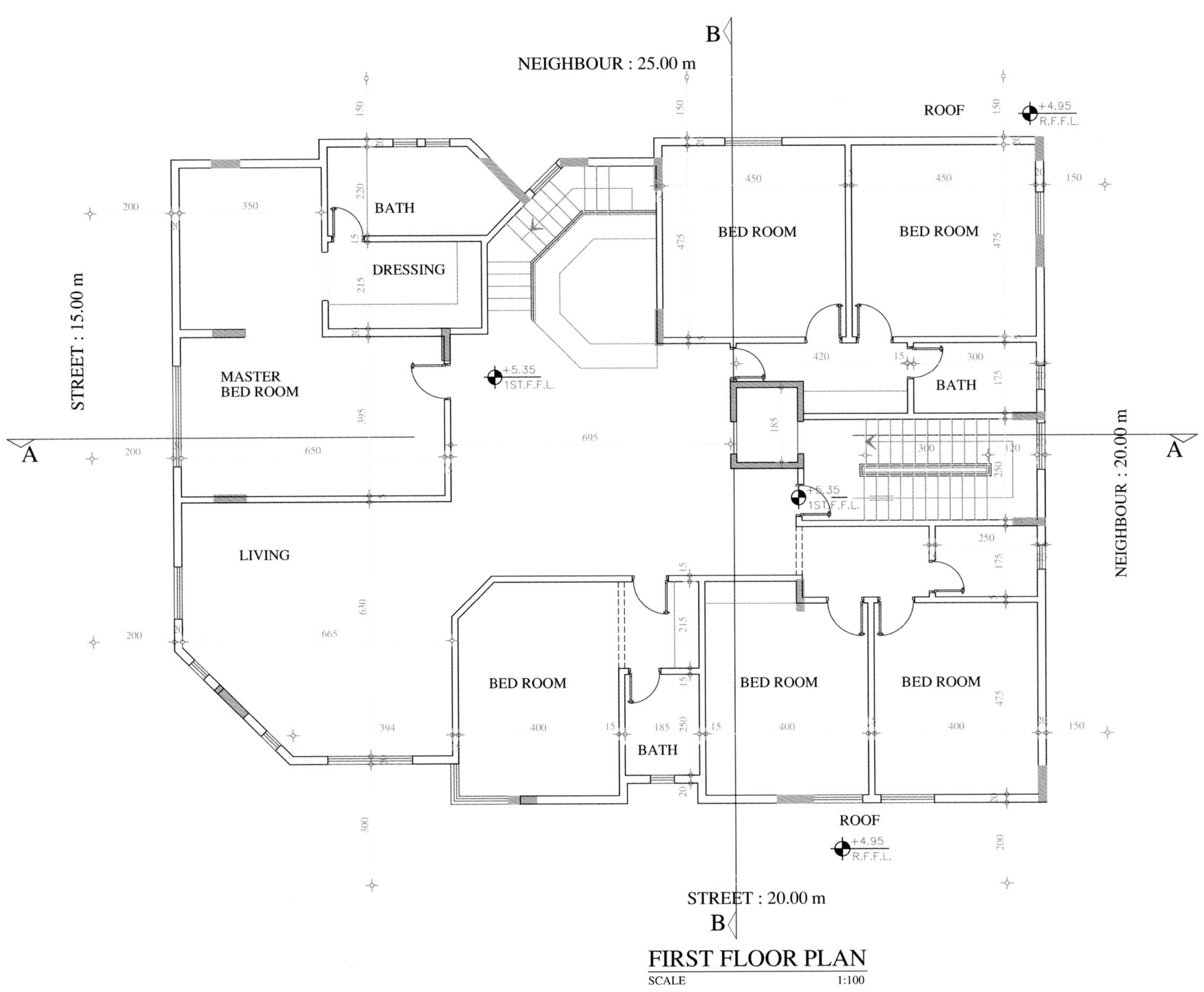

FIRST FLOOR PLAN

SCALE 1:100

INTRODUCTION

—Nada Faris

This project is the brainchild of my creative partner Maha Alasaker. When she arrived in the United States, Americans asked about her place of origin. "Where do you come from?" was then followed by a series of stereotypical questions: "Do Kuwaiti women cover their hair? Are they allowed to drive automobiles? Do you own pet camels?" Maha indulged these questions until one night she ran out of patience and blurted, "Just Google it!"

She felt in that moment the kernel of a creative project stirring. Instead of reacting curtly, she would depict Kuwaiti women for the outside world. The question was how? How does one go about capturing authenticity, or vulnerability, or intimacy of Arab females for a Western audience without Orientalizing the locals? And what is Kuwaiti identity, anyway? What makes Kuwaitis a different type of Arab? Or Kuwaiti females a different type of citizen? Are they?

Because Maha is a visual artist, she thought in terms of location. Kuwaitis live with their parents until marriage. They leave family homes to move in with spouses. Twenty years ago, Kuwaiti siblings lived in the same bedrooms. A strong oil economy, and an even stronger welfare policy of distributing national wealth among citizens, enabled Kuwaiti homes to expand. More rooms were built to accommodate the needs of individual sons and daughters. Simultaneously, families shrank. Our parents' generation is known for having an average of eight to ten children. This number dropped to half that amount. These changes allowed sons and daughters to discover privacy. Eventually, they received locks to bedroom doors.

When the private bedroom was first built, daughters left their doors ajar. In conservative families even boys were forbidden to lock their rooms. "Bedrooms tell many stories," says Maha. That was true for our parents' generation as well. What makes bedrooms today special, however, is their function: they now serve as sanctuaries for boys and girls who continue to grow in Kuwaiti families where collective needs outweigh the individual's. Families gather in living rooms, or at kitchen tables over breakfast, lunch, and/or dinner; they gather at family-owned beach houses or cottages in farms; on weekends, Kuwaitis gather at aunts' or uncles' or grandparents' homes. Presently, bedrooms in Kuwait provide a unique space for individuals to discover themselves.

Maha started this project in 2015. She emailed her immediate circle and sent messages to friends and family members who might approve of having their pictures taken for a Western audience. Most agreed until they learned that they were not going to dress up for these photos. Maha insisted on makeup-less faces and on casual attire. Perhaps the most shocking request was staging these images in private bedrooms. Once everyone heard these conditions, they backtracked.

She had no one to photograph back in Kuwait. While eating lunch with the family on National Day before heading out to her aunt's farmhouse, Maha asked her sister if she would be willing to pose in her *dara'a*, a loose gown that Arab women wear at home. It took ten minutes, because she already knew her sister's angles. When she returned to the United States, Maha developed the images and recognized the shape and contours of the project. She also discovered that the objections to her exhibition stemmed from a misconception. Because Maha sought to showcase an intimate aspect of the women of Kuwait, the candidates presumed she meant sleazy pictures in lingerie. After a few close friends followed in her sister's footsteps, Maha was able to share visual samples on her social media. The images comforted the viewers. Henceforth, people outside of Maha's immediate circle began contacting her and expressing interest in the gallery. By the third year, Maha had more offers than time to shoot them.

When she started, Maha hoped to reflect the various substrates of Kuwaiti identity. She wanted women who wore different variations of the veil as well as women who donned miniskirts and loose denim pants, women who belonged to various social classes and who experienced varied religious upbringings, those who were affluent and those who were impoverished, and the list went on and on, until it collapsed once Maha recognized the spirit of the exhibition. It was more about the will and freedom to participate than about being a visual depiction of socioeconomic categories and political or ideological labels.

She premiered the photographs in New York. Viewers' response and engagement motivated her to explore a different direction. Towards the end of 2018, I received a call. Maha wondered if I might be interested in adapting her gallery show as a book, specifically, to write the pieces that accompany the selection of images. I said yes without hesitation. I was on the lookout for a project that would catapult me out of my comfort zone, and Maha's *Women of Kuwait* encompassed delicious ingredients. I had to interview twenty-five women in a way that would expose me to their most authentic selves. This generally went well, but there were occasions when my candidates resisted the process. And why wouldn't they? I was a stranger, for all intents and purposes asking them to let down their guard, and to remove the masks they wear to hide their flaws. Their defense mechanisms served them to navigate Kuwaiti society without conflict. Yet here I was, forcing them to reveal the very parts of their beings that they reserve for intimate partners or best friends, and sometimes only for themselves. In return, I would splatter that vulnerability onto pages for other strangers to devour. One interviewee cried three times during the hour-long conversation.

"How are we feeling?" I inquired after I stopped the recorder.

She sighed, touched the side of her neck, and said, "I feel attacked!"

I would be lying if I failed to acknowledge the depth of the impact the process had on my psyche. I found myself continually transformed, my initial expectations and, in some cases, actual judgment or reservations, shattered, and my heart softened after each interview. The responses I received from the candidates are similar. During the discourse, I often asked probing questions that made the women rethink aspects of their lives. After the intense back-and-forth, I was frequently sent messages along the lines of "Thank you, that was informative," or "You have made me see the past in a different way."

If it does nothing else, I hope this book acts as a reminder that what we see at a first glance, regardless of the angle or the setting or the surrounding props, can never show us a person's inner truth—the accumulation of meaningful moments, challenges, memories, and goals that shape one's sense of self at a certain stage of one's life. There were women who changed completely after Maha took their pictures.

"Does it matter," said one of them before the interview, "that I no longer identify with myself in that photo?"

"No," I assured her. "Whatever we capture today will be as fleeting. I only ask that it be real."

Stylistically, I decided to write all the stories in the second person and in the present tense to complicate the very binary of subject/object and of time itself. Because Maha wanted to point the camera lens into women's bedrooms, I aimed to re-create some of the most intimate, vulnerable, unadorned moments in these women's lives, and instead of inviting the reader to learn about them from a distance, I strove to merge the viewer with the Other being observed. Finally, I wanted to collapse time itself by allowing the reader to experience these moments as though they were unraveling instantaneously. In some stories I focused more on elongating scenes and on drawing out metaphors. In others, I prioritized chronology and narrative. In all of them, I aspired for depth and truth. Yes, we are all in a state of flux. What mattered to me in each chapter was to capture with my pen what a camera might snap with its lens. And because I am primarily a poet, I focused on sound and emotions and images, and their relationship to one another.

Because we are women who live in Kuwait, we share similar challenges. We are still haunted by the trauma of the Iraqi Invasion at the end of the twentieth century. We are still coached against emoting, especially over losing our loved ones. We still grow up in homes where the tension between modern and liberal tendencies clash, sometimes violently, with more conservative interpretations of identity. We still develop tendencies, habits, and passions that are alien to our society. And almost everyone has a story of how their parents sacrificed their happiness in fear of what "The People" might say. I wanted to be fair to the women individually by writing about moments that shaped them, but I also had the book as a whole in mind, and I knew that I did not want to write, for instance, twenty-five stories about the impact of the war, or about losing a parent, or about the missed opportunities in life, such as those experienced by women who were forbidden from studying abroad. Therefore, I curated an array of moments that were both meaningful to candidates individually and provided variety and breadth as a unified collection.

On numerous occasions, I had to write around topics because candidates refused to share intimate moments on the record. Kuwait is a cocktail of clashing families. Regardless of how crucial the role certain events and encounters in molding the identities of the women in this book, most refused to incriminate family members, friends, neighbors, or even colleagues. Rarely did they agree to point a finger on the record, or even share something that might be misconstrued by the community. We spent hours discussing mental illness, family breakups, abuse, fraud, disappointments, and an equal amount of time blathering about love, romance, and unconventional friendships, about travel and adventures, and about the finer things in life—only a fraction of these memories appear in this book, for the reasons stated earlier.

I hope this project is seen for what it is: an artistic and/or poetic endeavor to capture an angle of female identity in Kuwait in visual snapshots as well as prose. This is not a project pretending to elevate a particular type of femininity or of Kuwaitiness. It is not an exhaustive list of all the categories of women in Kuwait. It is also far from claiming objectivity or neutrality in selection. After all, Maha and I are both artists. Our visions determine the elements we highlight and draw into the foreground, and those we overlook or push back into the shadows.

We hope you enjoy the book.

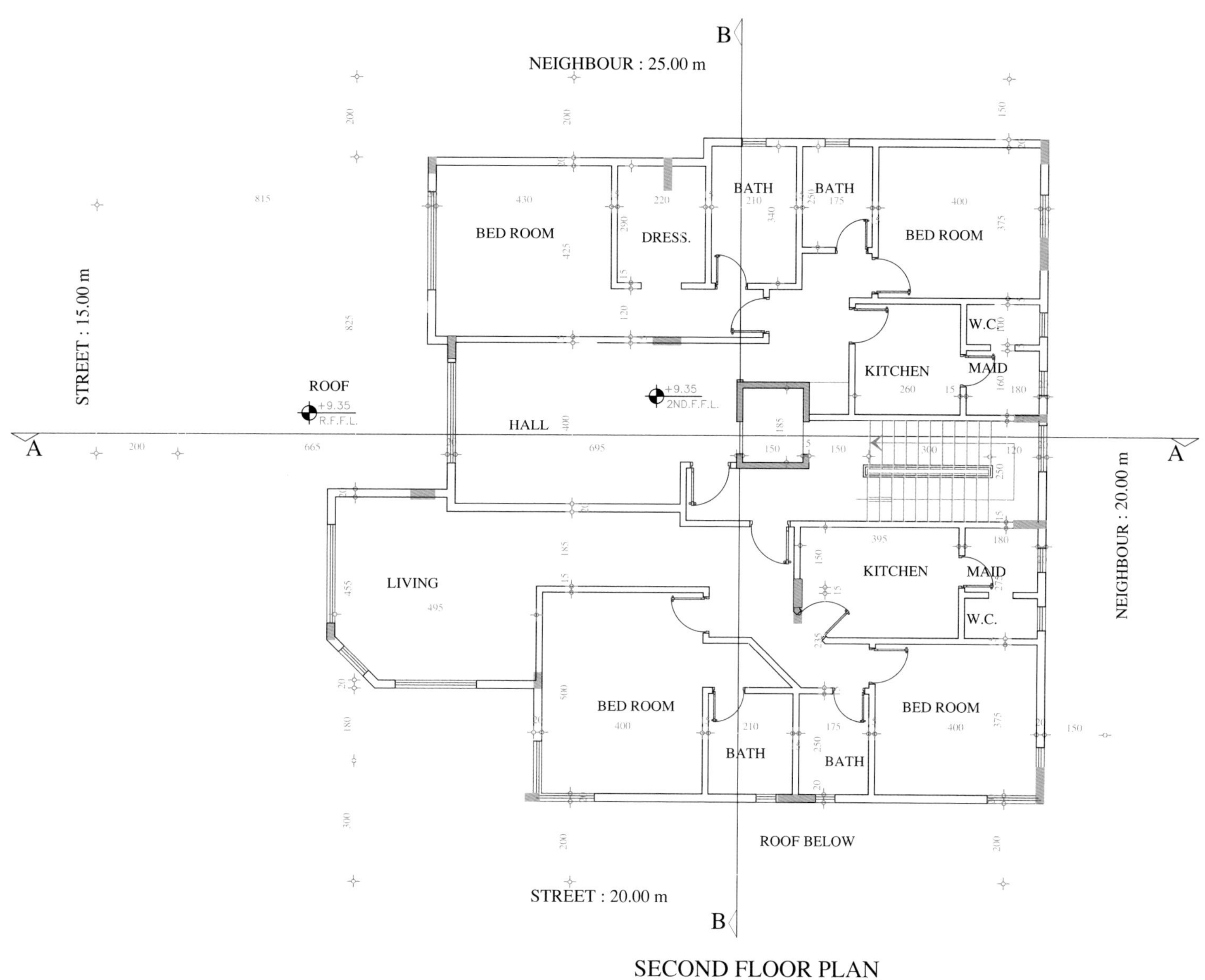

SECOND FLOOR PLAN

SCALE 1:100

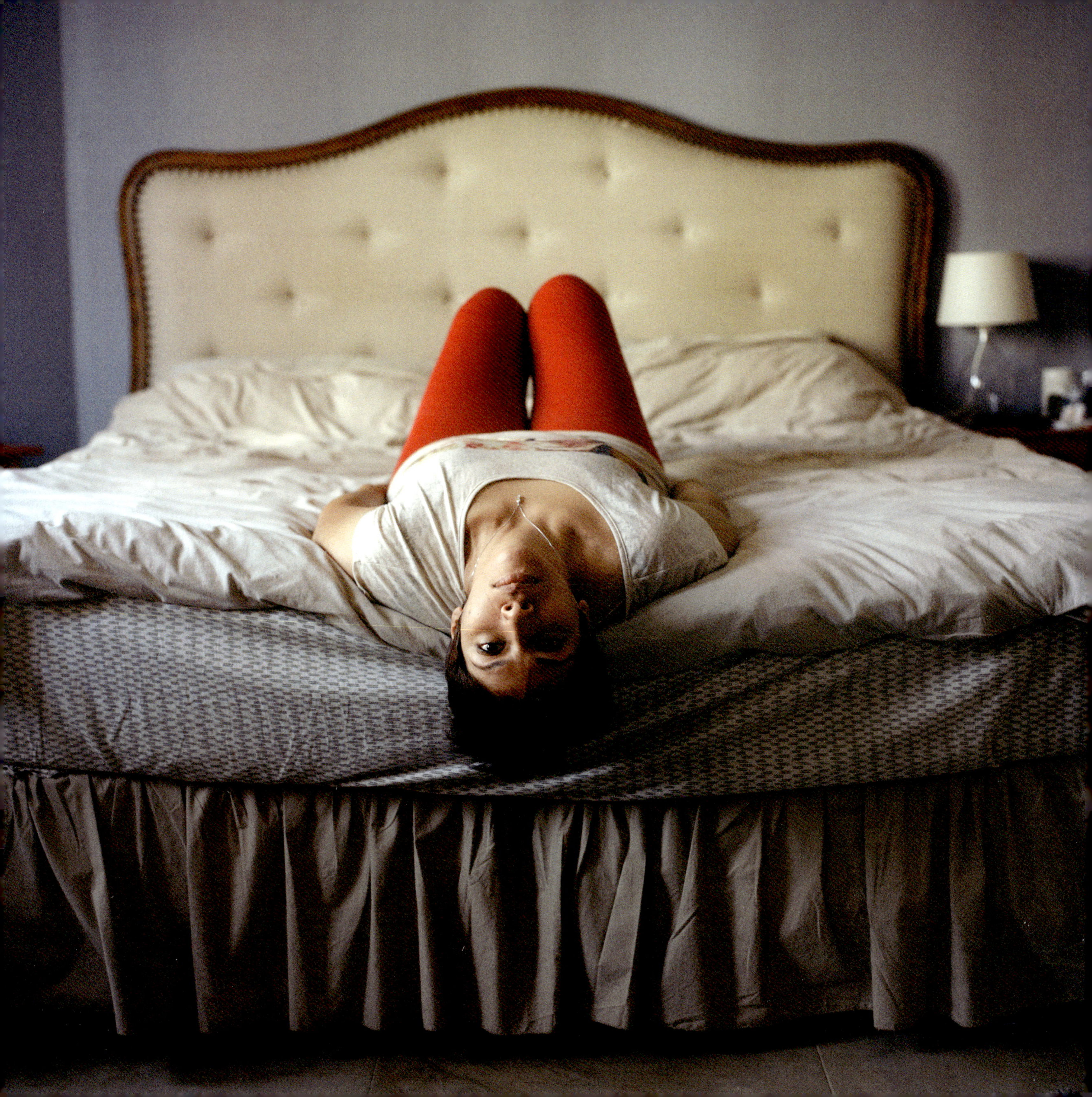

ATHOOB AL-SHUAIBI

Mangoes

You disagree with your mother. She thinks good parenting equals martyrdom. You always remember the mangoes. Whenever she buys them, she cuts up the fresh flesh and hands the pieces out to you and your siblings. She keeps the dry, brown slabs for herself. You love your mother deeply, but you also wonder, Why had she resigned herself to be like everyone else? Why did she give up on her dreams so easily? Did she even have any, outside of building a loving home?

Your aunt Lidia, on the other hand, is someone to admire. Unlike the other Kuwaitis around you, she never hired a domestic worker. To you she represents an alternative to typical Kuwaiti families. You promise yourself that when you set up a home, you will follow in her footsteps and raise your own children without a maid. You also look up to Lidia for her talents. She lives in a masterpiece of a home covered in mosaics, shards of broken mirrors glued into images and motifs, every room a work of art. The two-story house in Qadsiya announces its quirkiness from a distance. And she did it all herself, part by part.

But when your mother passes away, you inherit her photographs. She was an artist as well, and it dawns on you, on the bed, with all the snapshots of a happy life spread across the width and breadth of the mattress, that it was she who inspired your journalistic drive. It is hard for you to fight back the tears. Large wet drops fall on open mouths, wide grins and laughing faces. You wonder how a photograph can possess opposite properties. Even those that supposedly capture eternal joy can lead to intense bouts of weeping when encountered on other occasions. You had no intention of pursuing a higher degree when your husband picked up and traveled to Europe, with you and your daughter, to continue his education. Only now, you look up and the full implication of the sign you have hung up on your wall hits you like a gust of wind: "I wanted to change the world, but I couldn't find a babysitter." It was funny when you were raising the girls. Not anymore. You feel your mother's life force thrusting through your veins, motivating you to raven the flesh of life.

Since your daughters are moving on to college, you will have nothing to hold you back from bulldozing your way to the top. There is only one catch. The sudden realization that you are a replica of your mother carries with it a darker promise. Your mother's life was stolen at the age of fifty-two. You are forty-one. You cannot help but obsess, now that you are ready to live to the fullest…how much time do you actually have?

DEEMA AL-GHUNAIM

Time Travel

You are seven years old. You climb over a rock you call Grendizer because to you it appears massive. In your hand is a rusty piece of metal you refer to as a magical key that unlocks supernal ponds (puddles in the ground near your beach house where you play with your cousins). When your grandfather passes away in the last days of the war, your father turns his room into a library. Now you are eleven. You are in that library, traveling between worlds contained in pages. You write a note. You tear it up. You hide the parts between the books. You come across them fifteen years later and connect the pieces. You aren't sure what to make of the existential quality of the letter, which reads as though you are a soul describing the hand that you have been dealt. In the note you explain in the first person the family that you have been born into, the size of your body, your parent's social and economic conditions, and you can't help but wonder who you were writing for. An alien? Your future self?

You are thirty, in the passenger seat of a rental car. Your husband is driving down California's Pacific Coast Highway. You tell him to slow down, so you can take a picture.

The road trip reminds you of your father, a geomorphologist who taught you about the evolution of rocks and land forms by driving you around the Arabian desert to show you how sand migrates, how it changes color, from yellow to red, to purple, to black. He also explains why sand morphs across time and space. You put your camera on your lap. You pull out your travel diary and write, *Cars might be the closest things we have to time machines…*

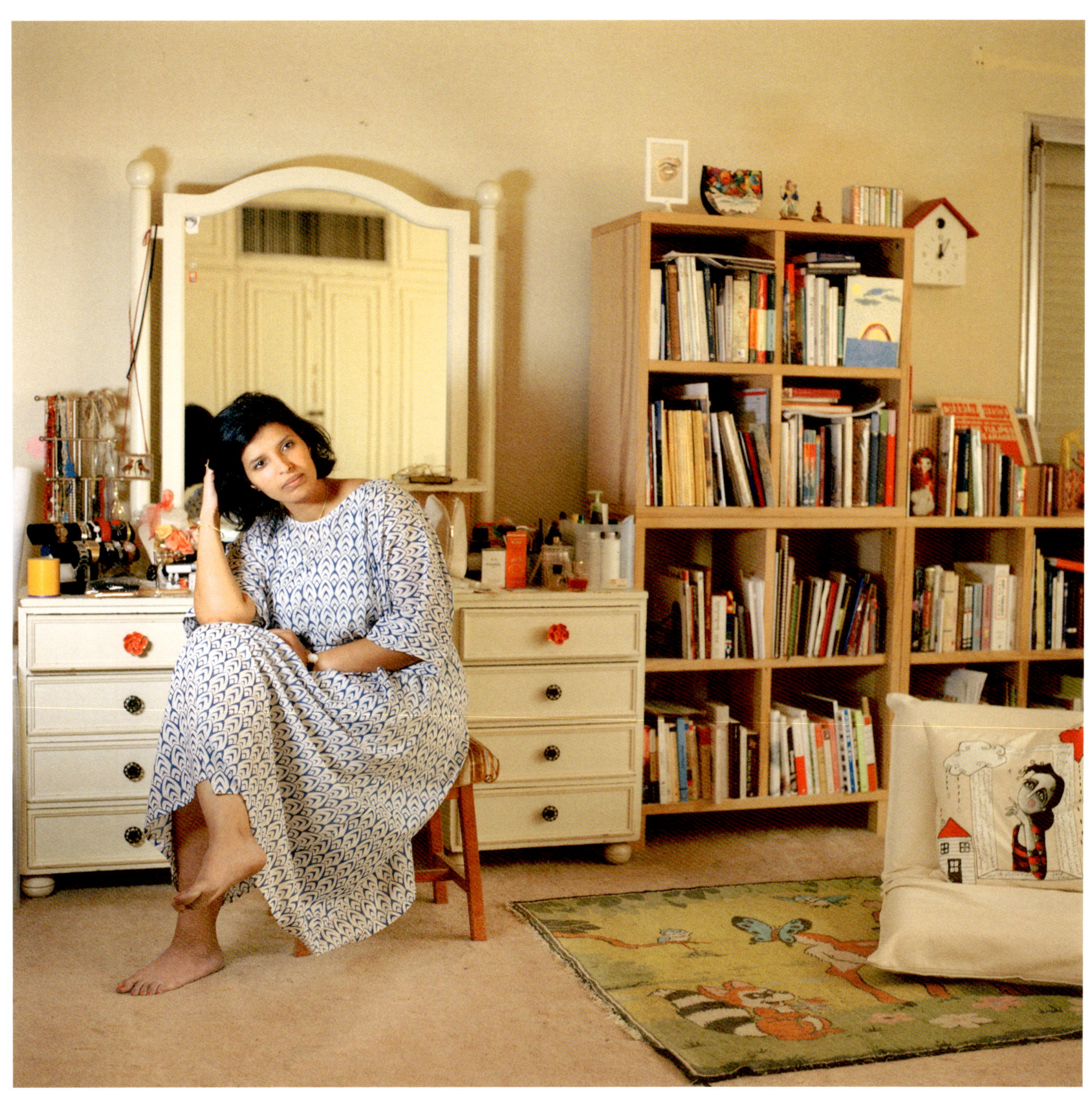

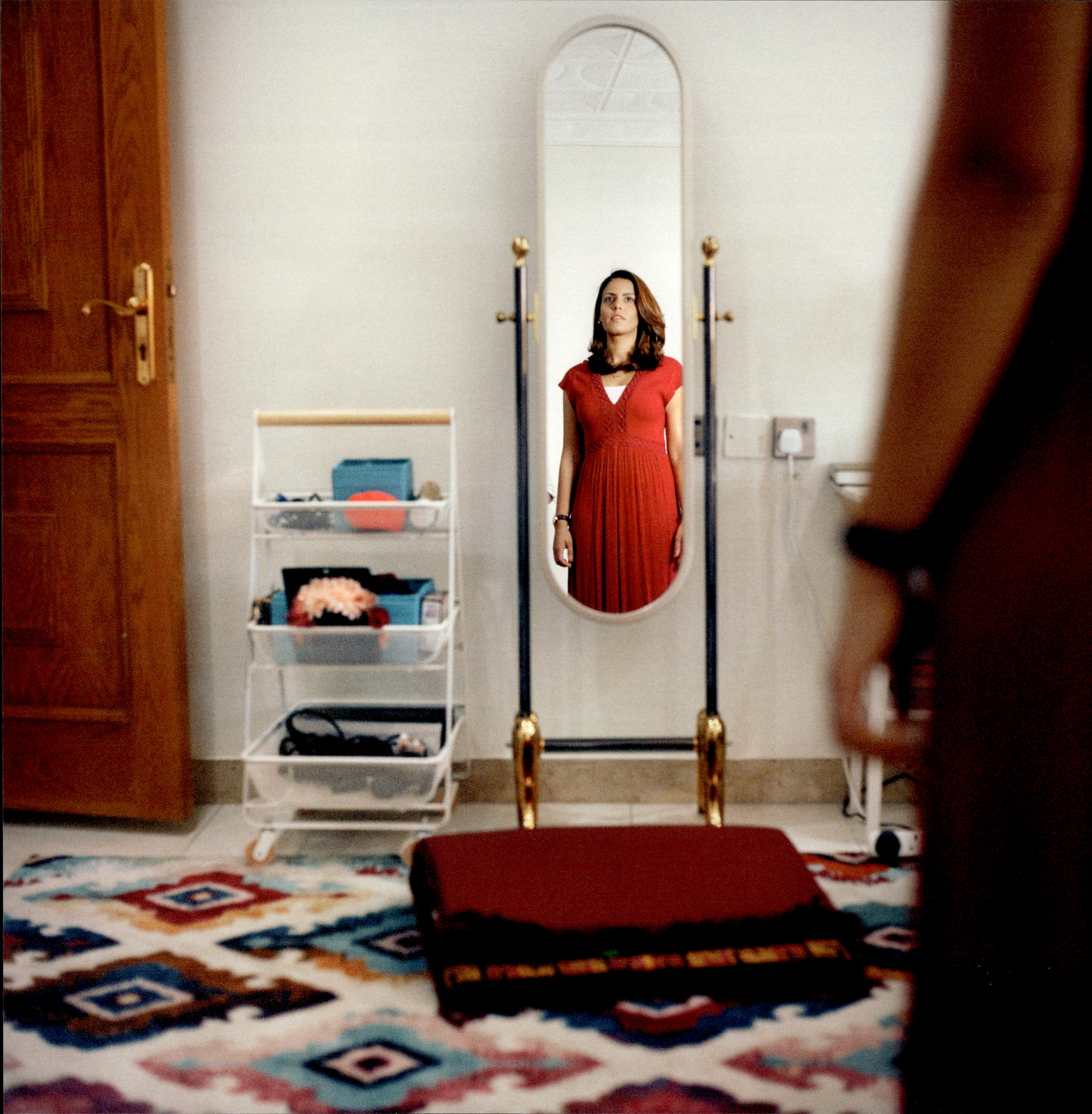

AMNA AL-MUTAWA

Reverence

Your feet touch the sill of a doorway. Beyond is the open sky, light blue, inviting. Below is a darker shade, the broad splendor of the ocean. Behind you is a man, attached to your body. Your friend jumped out of an airplane. Now it's your turn. You take a deep breath and leap into the air belting "I believe I can fly" at the top of your lungs. The wind muffles your screaming. Now you are falling, cracking open the bed of the sky and dropping fast. The man attached to your back launches your parachute. You stabilize. You are now hovering on the palm of the universe. Your friend is next to you, but you take in the view instead. All this ocean. All this openness. The wind is still caressing your body. The parachute is holding you in suspension. *God*, you think to yourself, d*o we ever stop to contemplate the beauty of our universe?*

Your stand in the same spot for eight hours. You are hunched over a refugee in a dentist chair. The old Arab woman has been mumbling her life story. Apart from the dental care all you can do is listen. What else can you say? "It's going to be all right?" Or "Hang in there?" You pull the mirror out of the old woman's mouth and let her know she's good to go. She invites you over for lunch. In the past you declined these offers, hoping to save their resources. Now you know the truth. It brings them pleasure to know you care, that you are willing to come to their shabby dwelling places, to eat of their food, to sit on the ground among their children, and to hear them articulate their pain. This one tells you she tried to flee her country on a boat eleven times and was caught by European officials patrolling the waters. They would detain refugees in a football field for days. Humiliate them. Scare them. Release them. They thought this experience would discourage refugees from escaping their war-torn country again. She informs you of her wealth. It's the reason she was able to afford the eleven attempts. She used to live in a mansion. She used to be rich. She had servants. She traveled. She drove expensive cars. Now she waits for you to finish your water so she can make you tea in the same cup. She reminds you that not everyone is privileged enough to be a refugee. The rest are simply collateral damage in this confusing war. You buy the family a set of cups before you fly back home.

You move your toes. Some of the sand that clung to them from the beach fall off in a sprinkle. You giggle. You made new friends, other medical professionals who decided to beach hop on a weekend in between volunteering at a refugee camp. You are lying next to a European man with an interest in astronomy. He is pointing at the dark night sky above. Wait for it. And true to his word, the first meteor rips through the sky, and you shriek! You hold your breath. Oh my god, you think to yourself, a planet that is on fire is gliding through the sky! And then you spot another one. And another. Your heart beats faster. A meteor shower. A sky full of burning rocks hurtling in every direction, and you, soft, small, lying on your back, underneath the mayhem. You realize the tears are flowing involuntarily. They drip and drip and drip down your face. Your chest starts heaving. Your friend turns to you and asks if you're OK. *God,* you keep muttering under your breath, *oh my God, thank you, thank you for keeping me alive long enough to see all this.*

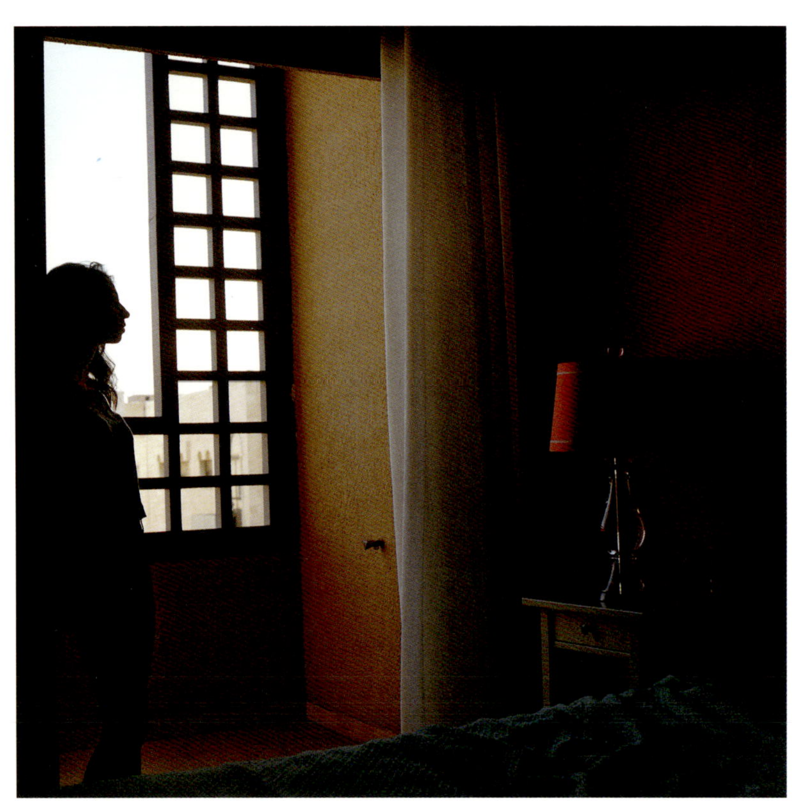

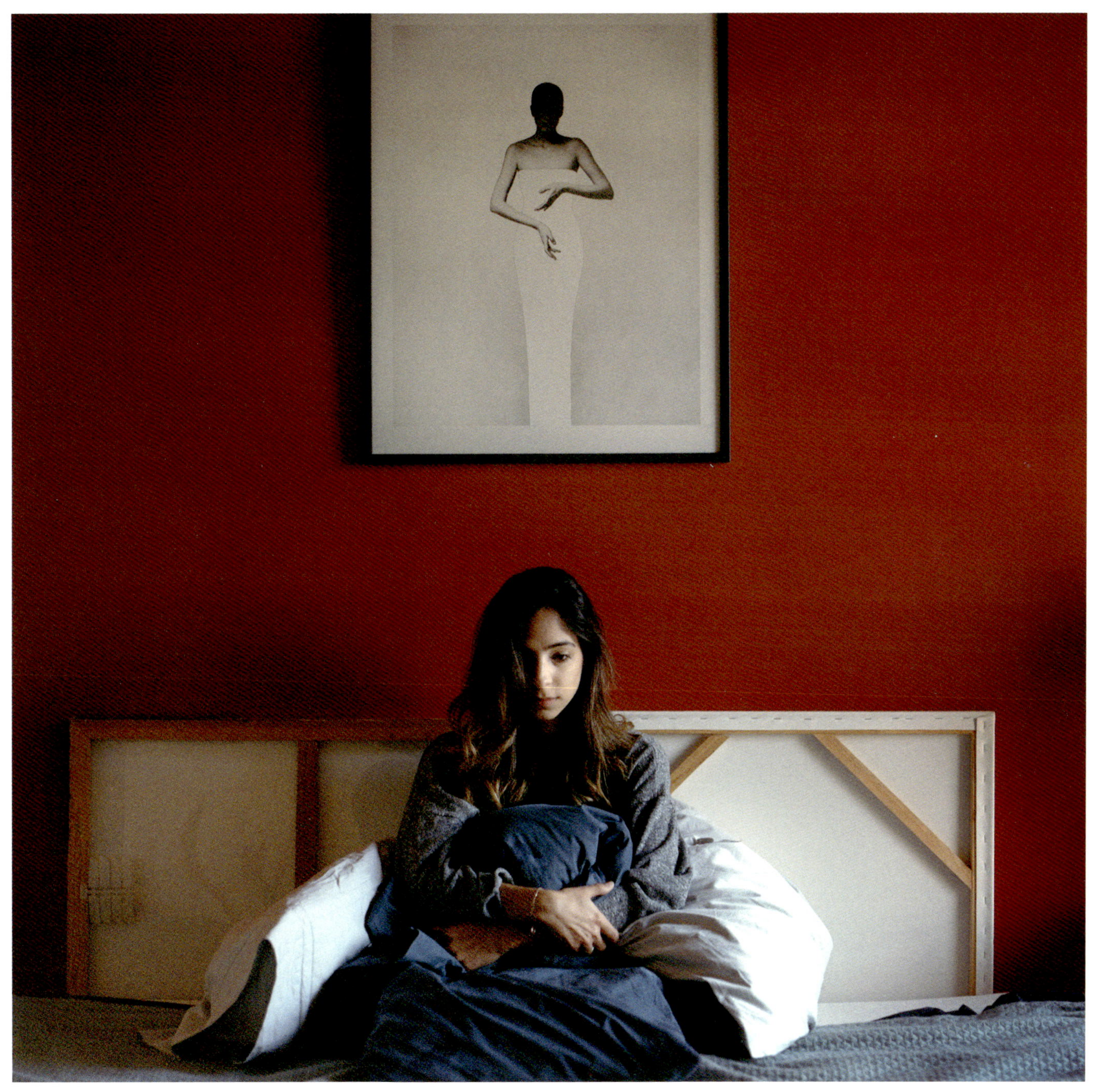

DJINANE ALSUWAYEH

Breathe

In a therapist's office, in Paris, you struggle to put your pain into words. The fact that you are expressing yourself in French, describing traumas of an Arab-Muslim upbringing to a Western professional, complicates the undertaking.

You are twelve years old when you meet Death. On the way to your horseback riding session, you are packed in three vehicles with friends and family. Your car arrives at the stables. Your friends' cars don't. Nobody teaches you how to grieve that loss. In fact, they caution you against weeping, "It will hurt the dead!" they claim, so you internalize your feelings out of respect. But those silly rascals bubble and bleed out onto the surface of every canvas you touch. You notice a pattern emerging. All the experts who judge your portfolios tell you there is a deep, weird emotion lurking in the depths of your soul. It aims to be known in your aesthetics.

After the third impactful loss, you break down. You are in a psychotherapist's office relearning how to breathe. The first few times are difficult. Your body fears the excess oxygen intruding in its veins and retaliates. The panic attacks scare you the most. You persevere until you see the difference it makes on your body, on your relationships with friends and family, and most importantly, on the way your breath filters light into memories of loved ones.

Now you know the value of speaking your feelings, of revisiting the traumas again and again, to vent it out, to shape it, to own it, and to share it with the world. You want to remind humans what it means to be complex emotional wholes.

You feel light, intact, like a feather floating in the breeze. You do not need anything beyond your knowing that you will land, eventually, back on your own two feet.

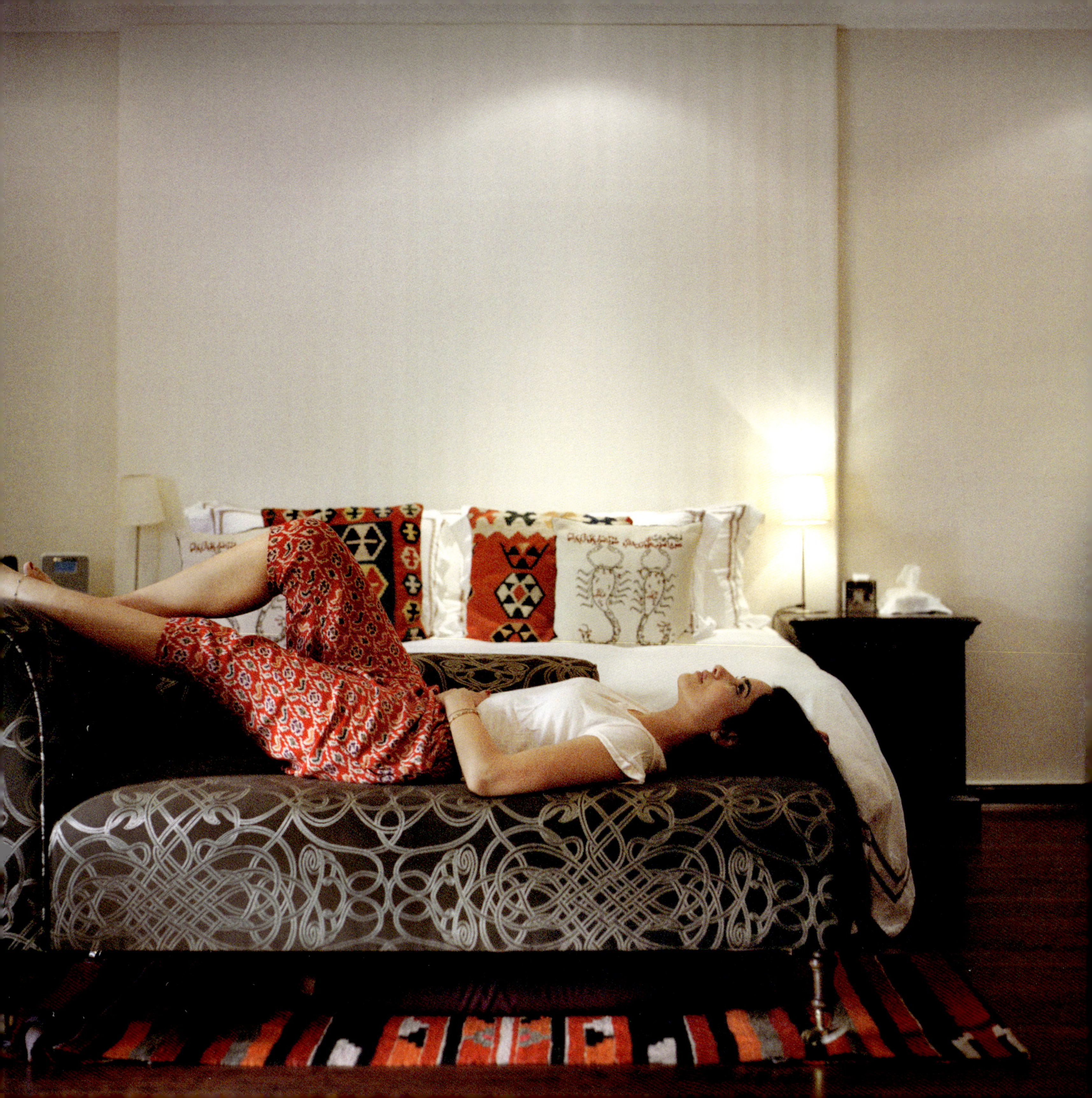

SHARIFAH AL-FALAH

Best Friend

Your best friend is a brown Pomeranian you call Scooby after your favorite animation. The youngest in a family of nine, you have learned to brush things off early. The dog sure helps. He lunges to your rescue when your father jokingly taps you on the shoulder, and he stops eating when you're sick. Your roommate in college at Arizona University and your human best friend is a conservative Muslim. She rejects your plea for a dog as a pet. You tie the knot after you graduate. You tell your husband you never want children. He tells you to forget about dogs forever. You do the opposite. You ask him every year, right around your birthday, if you can raise one together crossing your fingers the special occasion would soften your husband. But every year he says no. You do not lose hope, because your biggest no changes unexpectedly. You start praying for a little girl because you come from a family of mostly women. Your husband knows this too, so when you learn you are expecting, he bargains, "You name the boys, and I will name the girls."

When the boy comes out first, you celebrate. His name pops into your head as a memory from high school history class when you learned about a warrior king from Yemen. True to his name, Yazan comes out bold and rebellious. You spend every other school day apologizing to teachers and the parents of his classmates for his unruly conduct. And after eighteen years of saying no to the dog, your husband finally throws in the towel, when you explain that raising a puppy might help your son learn skills that made you lovable. So you roll up your sleeves and comb the social media platforms of different animal groups in search of a pup. You hear about a woman seeking a forever home for a two-month-old Shih Tzu. When you put in your request, she tells you not to get your hopes up, because you are the fifth caller. You break down. You weep and promise to love this puppy forever, describing the impact dogs have played in shaping your life. She remains steadfast.

You are in the kitchen baking chocolate chip cookies for your children when the phone rings at last. The woman on the other end screams, "Congratulations! You are now the proud parent of Luna!" But when you go down to retrieve your newest family member, palpitating with joy and anxiety mixed together, you take one look at that milky white-and-brown ball of fur and go, "No. Not a Luna. Definitely a Cookie!" You swallow her in a bear hug, and the image of your father flashes in your mind's eye. Your heart fills with warmth. After a while, you receive a phone call from Yazan's teacher. Instead of the usual complaints, this time she says, "Thank you, and please thank Cookie for all of us. She turned Yazan into a wonderful new boy."

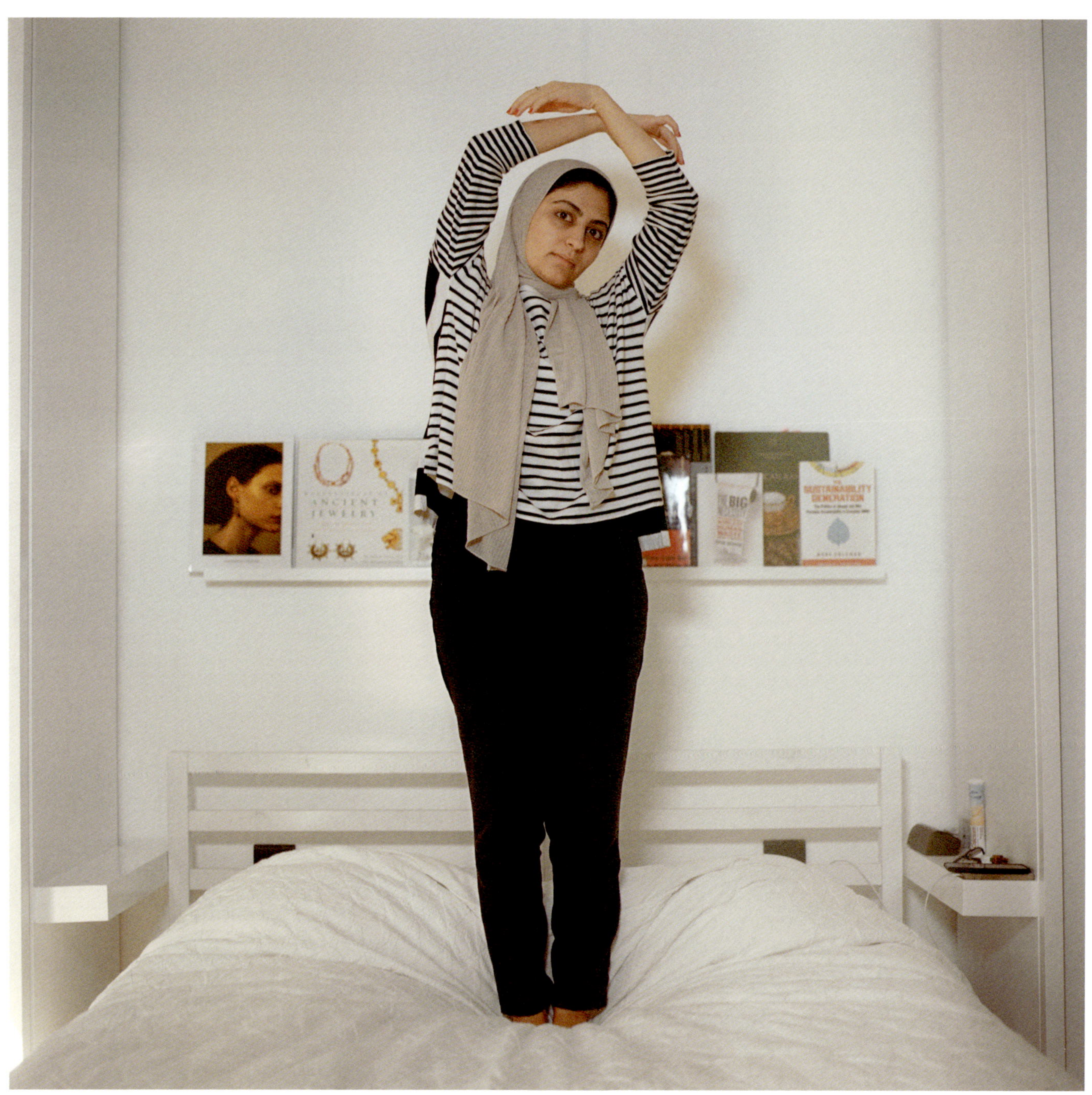
ANCIENT
JEWELRY
SUSTAINABILITY
GENERATION

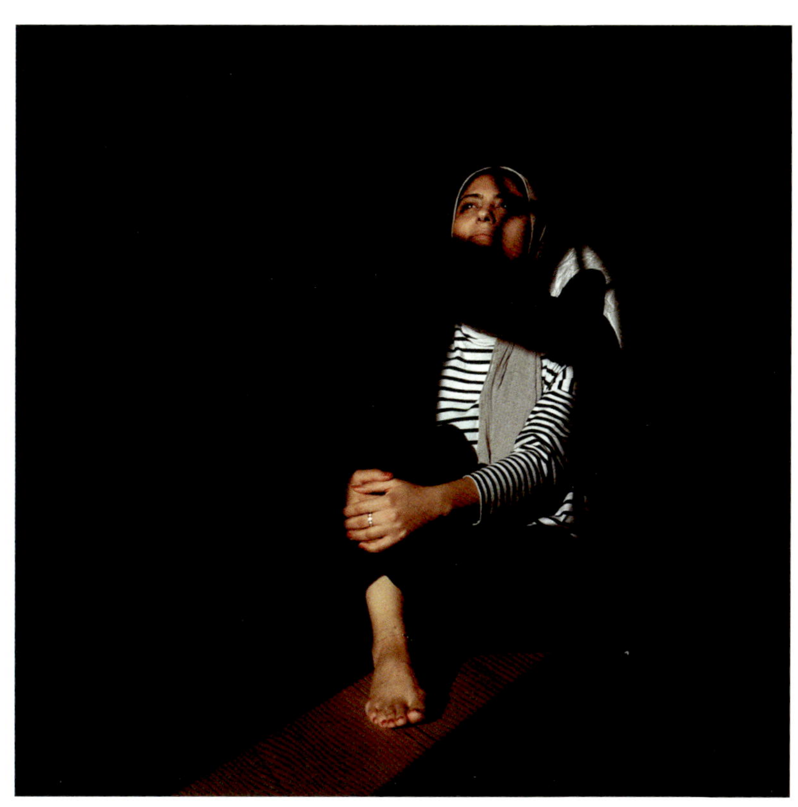

HAWRAA AL-MAQSEED

Invasion

When your eyelids drop, a bomb detonates. You turn to your right. You stretch a seven-year-old arm under the blankets, and search for the body of your younger brother. You are staying in your grandmother's house. Your parents and older siblings call from Germany after war breaks out in the middle of the night. "Keep your brother safe," they tell you. They will return when your mother completes her cancer treatment.

In the morning, you tremble into the yard with broomsticks to clear away the profusion of shrapnel and the dirt that follows explosions. Your grandmother calls you into the living room to deliver her instructions. "Your aunt's husband," she says quietly, "is a policeman. The Iraqis are rounding them up and killing them. We have to hide him here. We have to destroy his belongings so we can lie about who he is. You cannot tell the soldiers any of this, OK?"

You need a chair to reach the sink. Your seven-year-old body is hunched over pots and pans. Your small hands are chafed from the scrubbing, but you cannot stop. The Iraqi army storms into the house. They ask about your uncle. Your grandmother lies. Your aunt lies. Your brother lies. You lie and act as though the body wrapped up in coverlets with the painted face is your ailing grandfather, not your uncle. Your stomach convulses until the Iraqi soldiers complete their search and leave your grandmother's house for the next one on the block. On other occasions, you hide him in a ventilation duct. When the invaders barge in without prior notice, you think for sure this is the end. But your grandmother blurts out that the man among you is a teacher, a civilian family member. She gives him a different name and you all run with the new scenario like a troupe of natural actors. The nightmares will haunt your frail slumber well into your adulthood. *What if they find him? What if they return again? What if the bombs explode when I close my eyelids?*

But you are still seven. You survive a two-month journey escaping Kuwait and reach the rendezvous spot in Iran. Not knowing whether your family members would live or die the next day, the womenfolk decide to unpack boxes full of jewelry and wear everything at once. They gather in the living room with piles of precious stones. Your aunts layer dozens of necklaces one on top of the other, and stack glowing bracelets up their arms until they hit their elbows. Once their arms are full, they share the rest with the younger girls. Underneath black clouds of death and terror rise the echoes of relatives' laughter, defiant in their joy. You wear the earrings and multicolored rings when they pass them around, and your love for gold is born.

THURAYA LYNN

Unboxed

You are on your stomach. Your uncle is teaching you how to draw a tiger. You are seven and stubborn, so you do not follow his instructions. He shakes his head. "You are doing it wrong, Thuraya." Oh yeah? You determine to develop your own artistic style by age fourteen.

You gravitate to artistic friends in high school. You challenge one another. You draw an empty circle and wait. Your friend fills it up with images. She gives you a hollow square in return. You color outside the edges. But in college you hit your first roadblock. You are told the edges are there for a reason. There are norms to be observed, a society to be honored, and a box to be filled from the inside out. You turn your pencil upside down and start erasing your own edges, every squiggle, every curl, every giggle that offends or shocks the audience, one by one, they camouflage into the background. All you wanted was to fit in the elusive box. Now you dip your paintbrush in black, in yellow, in pink, in green, but nothing comes out. Everything melts into white.

In the midst of your depression, you buy a cat. You know nothing of her needs. Nothing of her struggle. Nothing of the cruelty of the animal industry. You almost regret your decision until you spot the first burst of color splashing onto your living room wall. Then another. Then another. You squeal with delight, and this time, adopt a second cat. Your pets teach you to love life so intensely you never knew your heart could beat so hard. You watch them build a family together. And when you read on your social media feed that two kittens require immediate foster care, you react without thinking. You take them as other members of your growing family. You tell your husband your life is now motivated by the will to be of service. Everything you make, from this point onward, will be utilized to help animals in need. And when you're done declaring your mission, you stomp on that stupid box.

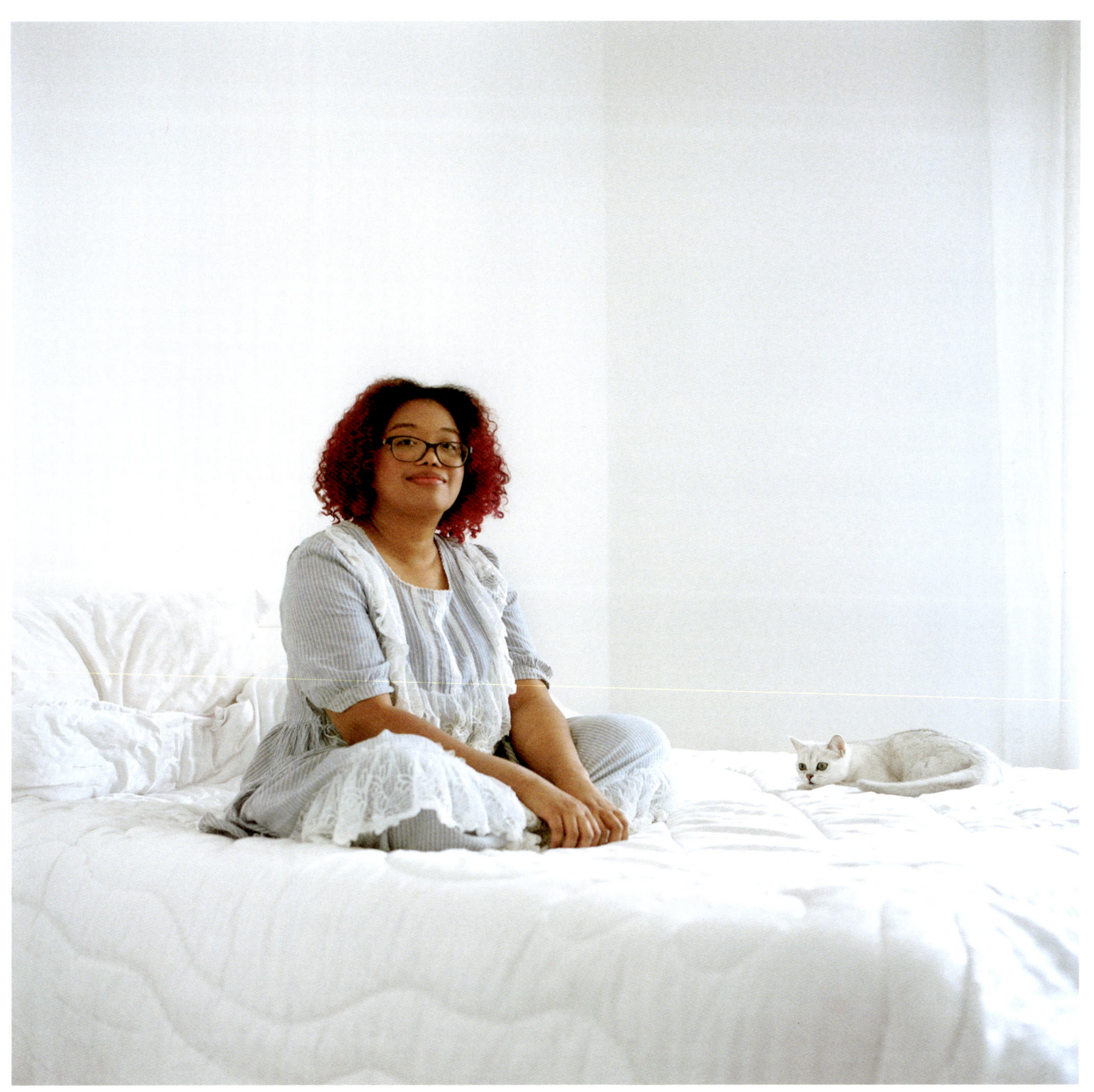

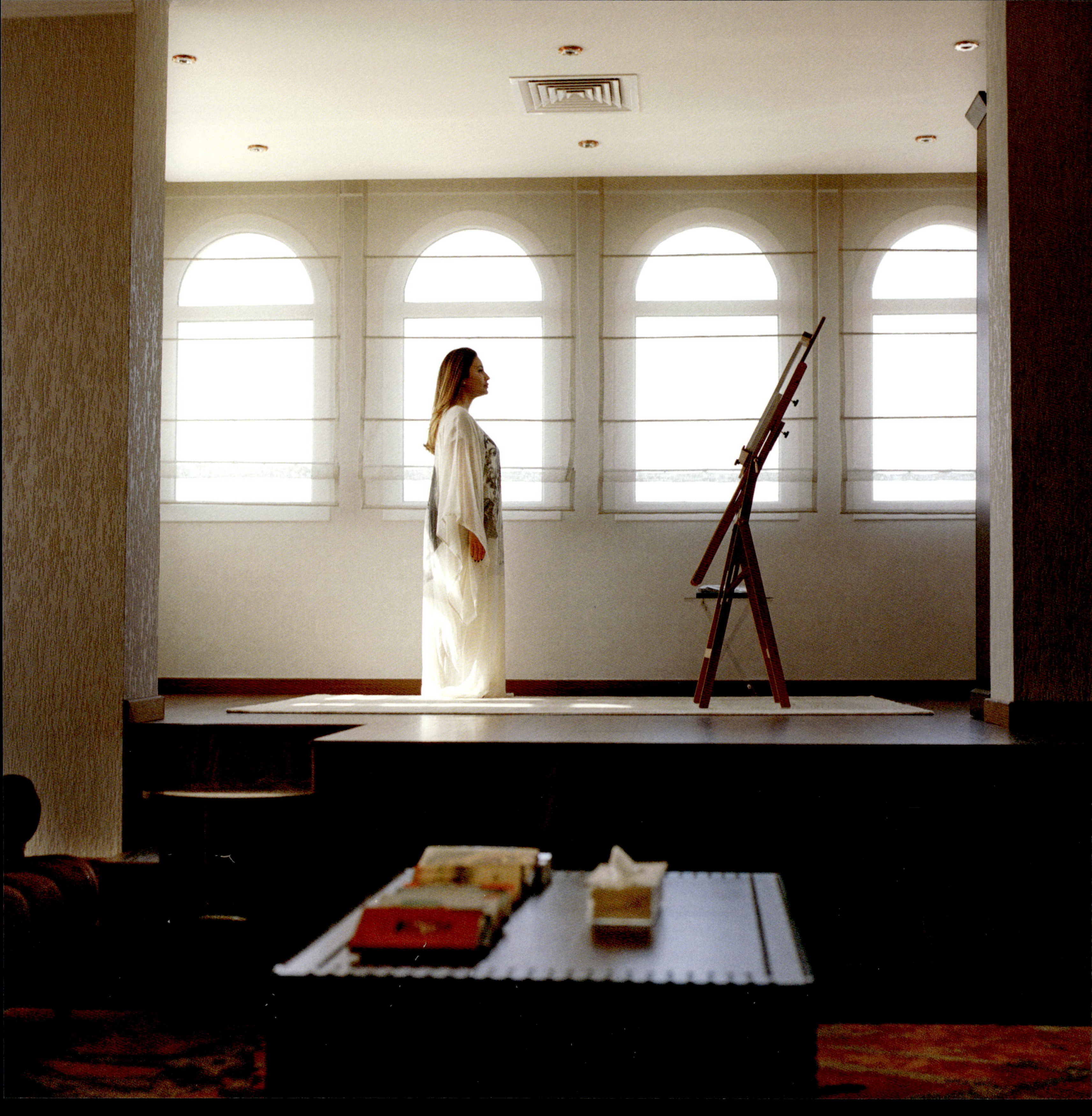

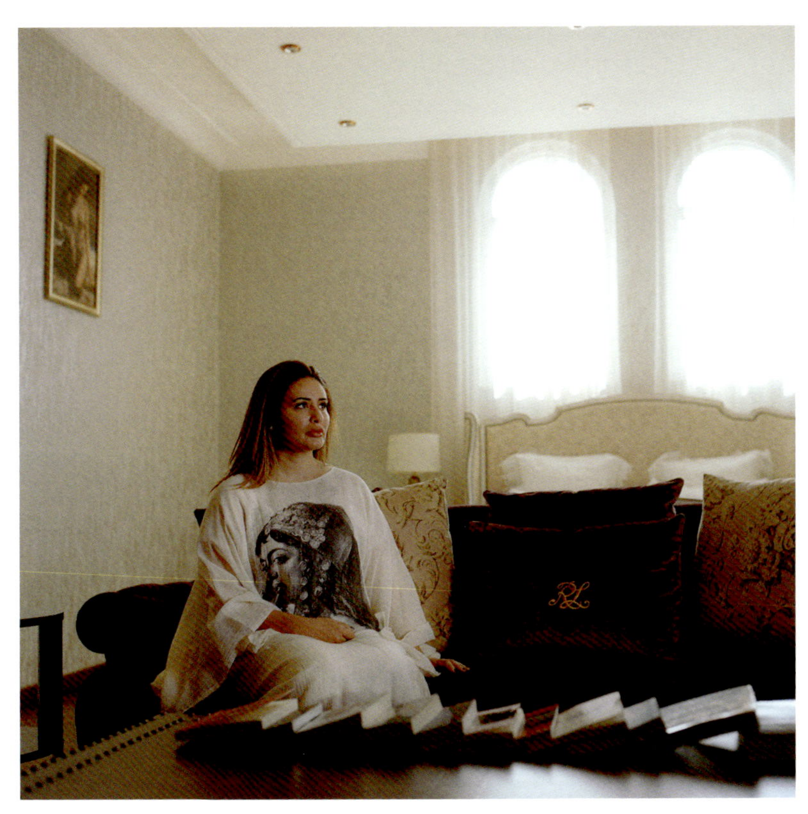

AWATIF AL-SABAH

Purification

You are walking on burning coals. You hear the loud shouts of encouragements echo all around you: "Keep walking!" and "You can do it!" You complete Tony Robbins' "Walk of Fire" and study more courses on self-empowerment. You receive certification in coaching and enroll in a master class, yet you continue to doubt yourself. Your Romanian trainer says something that catapults you into action: "It will be selfish not to share your knowledge with your community." *And you are not a stingy gal!*

You leap into the burning unknown. You establish a coaching office in Al-Hamra Tower. Your business grows. When your seven-year-old daughter tells you she thinks her hands are small, you remind her that the ability to change internal narratives is within our control. After a few weeks of uttering affirmations, she becomes a believer herself, then says, "Mama, I'd like to you to meet my friend, because she's tiny! Can you help her grow too?"

You chuckle. "It is not about changing our environment, but about transforming the way we think about experiences that leads to a healthy, fulfilling life. We can learn to be kinder and more powerful once we reclaim our thoughts."

And because you want to give back to your community, and life coaching, like self-empowerment courses, coalesces into expensive transactions, you partner up with a Brazilian friend to host a monthly Women's Circle at a public park, free of charge. You get fifty to sixty participants from all walks of life. A Persian woman who cannot afford transportation walks half an hour in the blistering heat just to catch the event. You all stand in a circle, equal in essence despite outward differences. You hold hands to strengthen the conduction of warmth. You take a deep breath and pray in one voice, "We give energy and support to all corners of the world. We are loved. We are cherished. We are strong." And after the bonding ceremony, after the tears and confessionals, after the human connections, you crank up the music and glow.

MARIAM AL-NUSIF

Self-Love

You think you comprehend unconditional love because you know how it feels when one is discriminated against based on superficial labels. People won't know this at first glance because of your name—and while this expectation is part of the problem, it doesn't even graze the pain of your upbringing. There were days you simply prayed for the kind of hurt that leaves you straddling this world and the next; only then, you were certain, would people penetrate the surface and take pity on your struggle. Unfortunately, Kuwaitis' love of social norms outweighs compassion, and so you were left with once choice: Stay and suffer until your final breath or muster the courage to perform the impossible and get out. Though your heart is beating maniacally inside your chest, you go ahead and trust in friends and family members and strangers, who help you attain your freedom.

Now you are back in the country bursting with energy. You desire to help as you have been helped, to give back to those in need, to protect everyone—damn it! You will not rest until you save the whole wide world from injustices and bias. You curate public spaces, bypassing the hindrances of bureaucracy so that small businesses can share their services with customers directly. You call it the Secret Garden because you want to build something magical. Your intention is to spread unconditional love, to bridge the gap between locals and expats in an area known for intensive othering. But while you extend a soft hand to the expat community, you still wake every morning to news of misdemeanors and pilfering.

It is only when you stop wanting to spread unconditional love that you realize you do not even know yourself. You have spent a lifetime hiding your flaws. You now commence with the knowledge that if you cannot recognize your own defects, then you are incapable of loving others—for mercy begins at home.

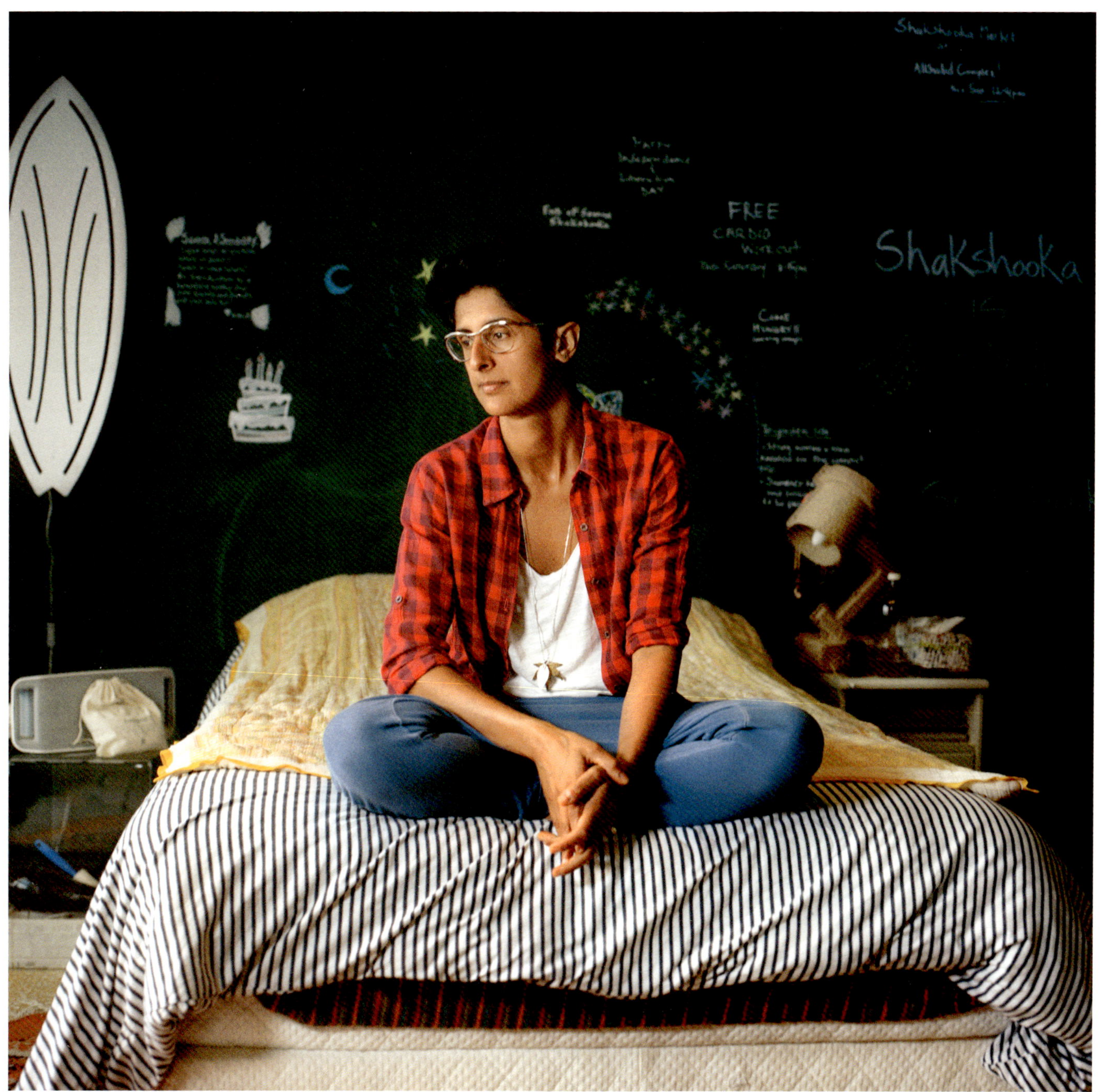
FREE
CARDIO
Workout
ShaKshooKa

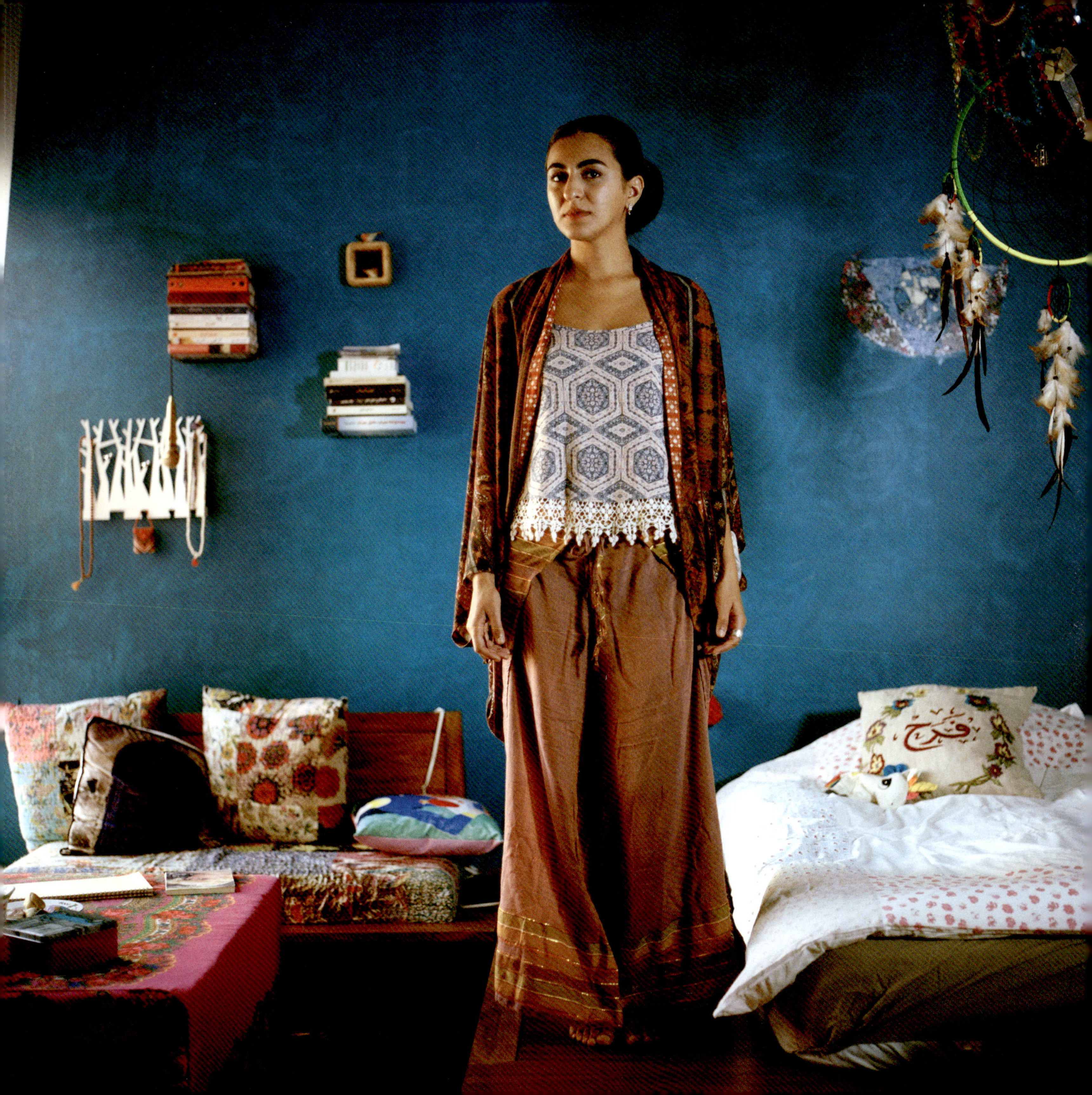
فرح

FARAH KHAJA

Mirror

Jalal Al-Din Al-Rumi, the Sufi poet, writes that "Truth was a mirror in the hands of God. It fell, and broke into pieces. Everybody took a piece of it and they looked at it and thought they had the truth." You are quivering in your bedroom. Because you lied to your mother about getting surgery, you think you have to struggle alone. When she asked you where you were going the previous night, you said, "To the dentist. My nerves hurt." Now you are writhing in pain you did not anticipate, and your domestic helpers aren't home. That's when your mother finds out about your surgery. She nurses you back to health. You always thought you were different. Now you wonder if you are perhaps two pieces of the same mirror that catches light at different angles. The recovery process takes you down memory lane.

You are on your way to Bayt Lothan with your mother. You sit on a large piano and dip into the beauty of melodious patterns. After the Invasion, your mother joins the Red Crescent as a volunteer, and after twenty-five years of aid and awareness campaigns, your mother has seen it all: death and violence, orphans and disabled children, poverty and natural disasters, prejudice and missed chances, as well as the endless wars—but she never loses her zest for life or love of travel. When she lands in Iran, she maintains a photo journal of the area and the inhabitants she meets along the way. Strangers become long-distance friends after earnest conversations and home-cooked meals.

At seventeen, you join your mother on an expedition. Dar Al-Athar Al-Islamiyya, where she has been a regular member, is hosting a trip to India. You are in your final year of high school, and though you do not yet know what you want to do with your life, you apply to public and private institutions. When you return, you find that you have been accepted to both. You choose the National Council for Culture, Arts, and Letters over working at the National Bank. Days later you learn that Dar Al-Athar is seeking employees, and you appeal for a transfer immediately. This is where you shine.

This sheen aligns with your mother's when she returns from Iran with carpets, handmade rugs that have seen the weaving of history play out on their surfaces, and you are building your own commercial business at the same time. You melt silver into rings and transcribe on the edges quotes by the Sufi poet, so you debut your products alongside your mom's, still wondering whether the pieces of the mirror will, someday, unite.

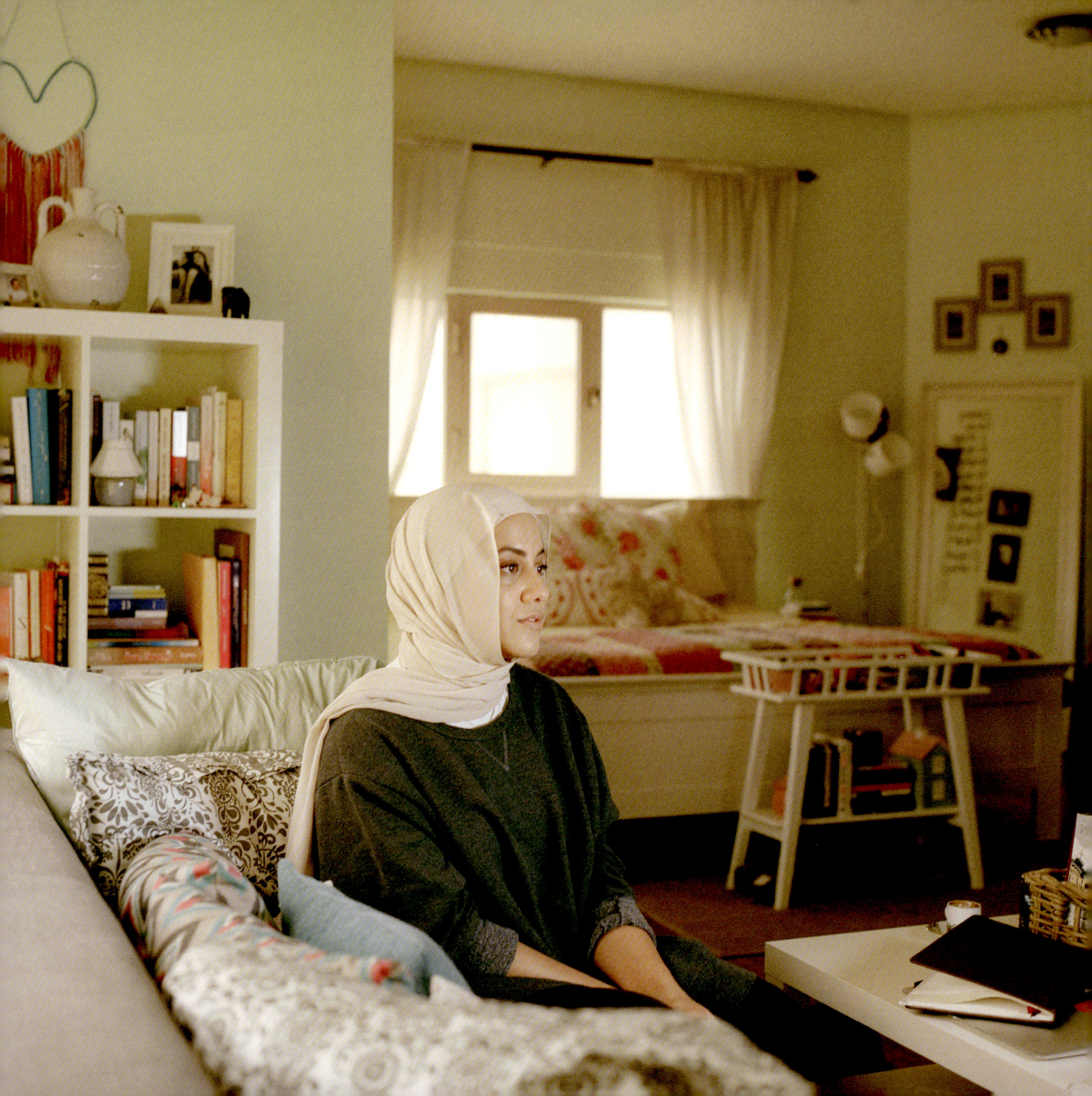

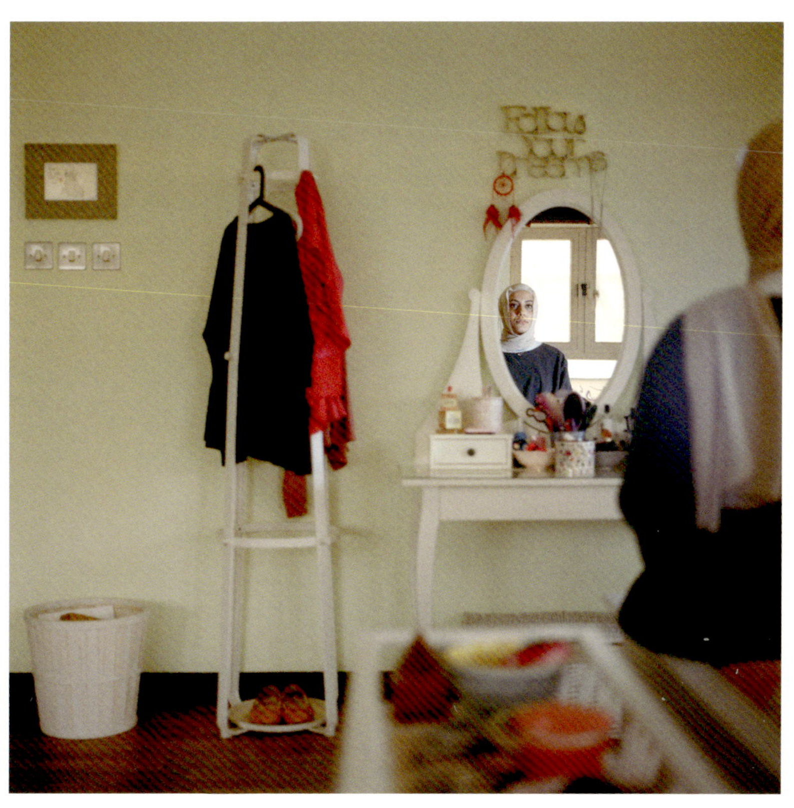
Follow
Your
Dreams

FATIMAH ALYAKOOB

Soul

You are listening to American soul music from the '70s. Your father is driving the family across beautiful vistas, rocky terrains, and verdant forests. You move from state to state and he points in this and that direction, describing his aspirations. It's almost like he knows something you don't. He says, "I want to buy a house here," and after a pregnant pause: "but I don't know if I have enough time."

Your father is diagnosed with brain cancer. Now you are in the U.S., not for a vacation, to acquire advanced degrees, or to visit family members, but for treatment. You and your mother are his caretakers. You wake him up two hours before his radiation appointment because you are unsure about his ability to cooperate. There are days when, in the midst of getting ready he refuses to leave, not out of malice or any ill will. He simply forgets days and decisions. So you plead. You beg. You barter. Your body crumbles under the exhaustion. You, who were never overweight, now spend most of your days in a hospital lounge dining out of American vending machines: Oreos, Diet Cokes, and Lay's are what you consume between radiation sessions and medical judgments. You barely have leeway to think of yourself, of your own needs, of rest, of health, of happiness. Society penalizes you for any stinginess of presence. They lambaste you—How dare you?—for spending two days in Dubai, or three in Turkey, when your father is dying in Kuwait? For two years, you are judged whenever you make the mistake of smiling at something. Your very humanity is questioned.

But before your father passes, the mother of your friend gives you the most courageous advice: "Never feel guilty for the relief you will feel afterward." So when it happens and you grieve, you also feel a burst of light. You trust that your father, the most amazing man in your life, who has been struggling for two years, is now in a better place. Your life completely changes from this point onward. You let society complain to itself. You simply stop engaging or indulging in the chatter.

Before the brain cancer, your father realized that he wasted his life working. He did not stop to appreciate the beauty of his surroundings, or the music of birds in the trees, or of fulfilling his own needs. When the emotional roller coaster that you experience upon your father's passing stops, you find yourself in the same spot, in the same car, listening to the same American soul music from the '70s, but now it is you who is behind the wheel, and you promise not to waste your time.

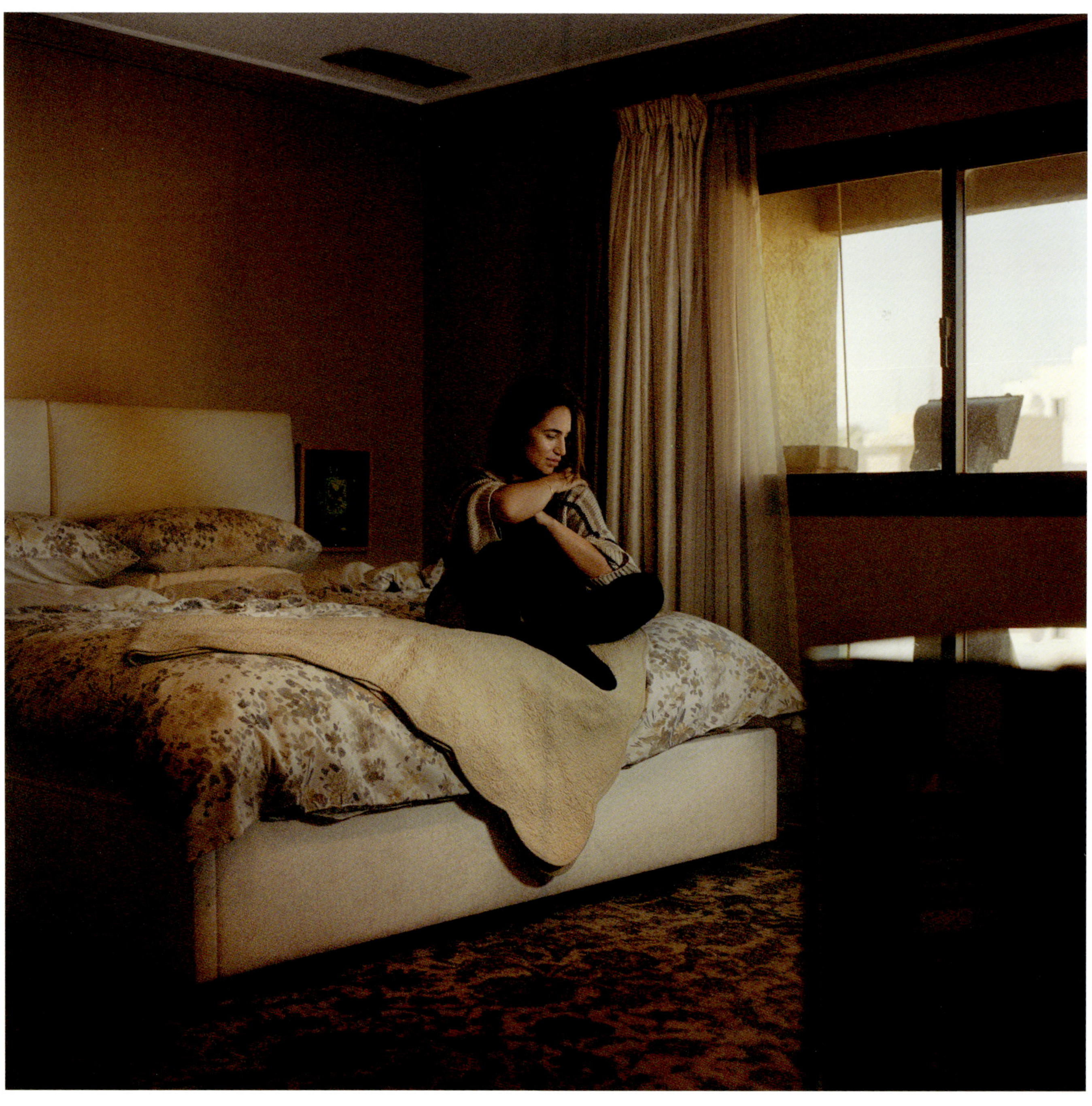

ABRAR ALEBRAHIM

Classical

You turn nine in the Islamic Calendar. In the Gregorian, you are still eight. Because your parents are conservative, they tell you to wear the veil. You are in Paris. Eight years old. In a veil. You promise never to come to this oppressive city again. "Do you want to go to Disneyland or to a theme park?" your parents ask. "Take me to the Louvre," you respond, "I want to see the Mona Lisa." But they say no. Some things contradict their belief systems. This includes art. You spend your life figuring out a way to bypass their guidelines. When they prohibit music, you ask them if they can permit the classical type. There are no lyrics, no gyrating beats, no friends that will be bopping up and down to the melodies after all. When they agree, you get know them by heart: Mozart, Chopin, Bach and Beethoven, they brighten your midnights, your evenings, and mornings. You push back, and back, and back until you are out of fuel.

You make the mistake of tying the knot too quickly, but you suck it up, you swallow your discomfort, you turn away from agreements that do not involve your input, you resign yourself to a life lacking in fireworks. You do your job until Imam Sadiq is bombed.

Your uncles prayed in that mosque, so when you see the images of the men and children lying in a pool of blood, in the middle of an act of worship, in the last days of Ramadan, something inside of you snaps. Now you can tell the difference between living and dying. You drive to court. You file your divorce papers. You pull off the veil and toss it onto the passenger seat. You keep your eyes on the road.

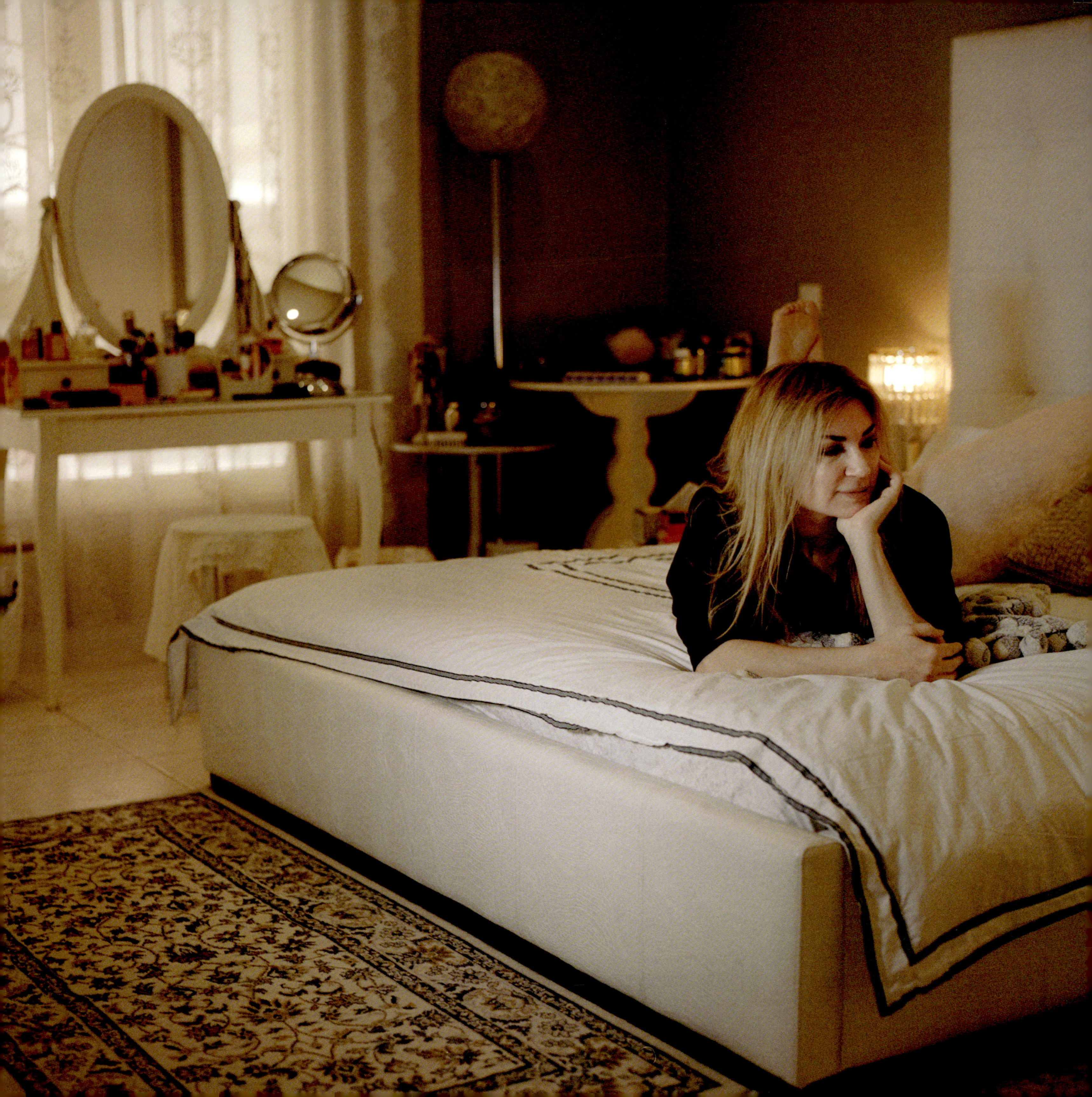

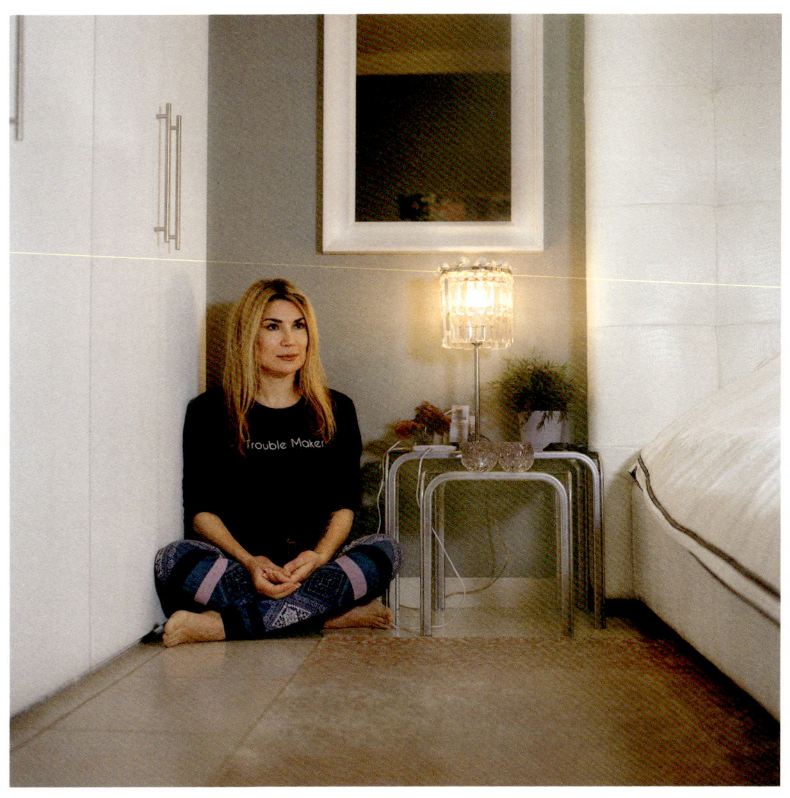
Trouble Maker

SHUROOQ AMIN

Submersion

You release your human senses in the depths of the ocean. Your vision bends and refracts as you adjust to the hues, the blues, the greens, the grays. Swallowed in the belly of the water, you listen with your eyes and watch with your ears. Your abilities switch and keep alternating. You flap your arms around to orient yourself, you kick your legs to elevate, to drop. You taste the zone. You relish the subtleties of living. Your heart is beating, you hear it through floating bubbles. The tentacled plant is swaying under your scuba diving boots. Schools of fish are commuting idly from one side of the ocean to another. You see them all, pulsing with vigor and life force. The same shock of red and orange and yellow that makes up the fire pumping in your chest. You test your strength, your courage. You grow your resolve and your muscles. This is not seeing the world upside-down. This is seeing through the façade of living, the veil that blocks the world from being perceived by the human spirit.

You transcend your human senses. In the middle of your studio, you sway to the rhythm, your headset is plugged into your iPod, your playlist is ready. You are preparing to dive into the empty canvas staring back at you, to front crawl over the blankness, to smear the subtleties of existence with a thick brush and a smudge of your fingertips. You want to belong. You want to swim like the indolent fish with the rest of your neighbors, but every time you paint a puzzle on that canvas you forget to attach the final piece in its place. You search all over the studio for your alter ego. When you find it, languishing on the side, it always dances a few inches away from your paint-covered reach.

TAMARA QABAZARD

Surrender

Your body is wrapped in a piece of fabric that is hanging from the ceiling of a gym. When you begin to swing, the images come one by one. You are two years old in a dance studio. It is your first day learning ballet, the initiation of a love affair with music and movement that will oil your bloodstream when the world turns cold. Now you are six years old. You stand next to a local man who throws a Pepsi can into an elephant enclosure in Kuwait's national zoo. You watch as the majestic beast picks up the soda with his long gray trunk and stuffs it in his mouth. Even at that age you think "This cannot be good for the elephant...," so you promise to become an "animal doctor" when you're older (because you have not heard the word "vet" yet). You are ten, standing in front of a mirror, facing a different type of beast: an eating disorder that reaches its peak in college, when your body loses so much weight you can't carry a backpack without crumbling. A good friend drives you to an in-patient facility in New York where you are pursuing a veterinary degree. Agreeing to the treatment is the best decision you make. It teaches you to relinquish the illusion of control the eating disorder provided. You forget about counting calories and about judging your body. Now you love it all. Unconditionally. When you return to your country you find employment in that same zoo that ignited your life's purpose. You are given an orangutan that has been smuggled through the borders. The criminal sneaking the ape into the country is caught driving under the influence. The orangutan is passed out in the passenger seat, high on drugs. You identify with that ape, wild and primal in meat and marrow, but here you are, the both of you, trapped in a habitat that challenges your survival. Your dedication and care pay off. The orangutan is finally rehabilitated and returned to his homeland in Indonesia. You focus to still the images. Your limbs hang loosely in the air. You appreciate the freedom that comes with surrendering control and simply being in yourself.

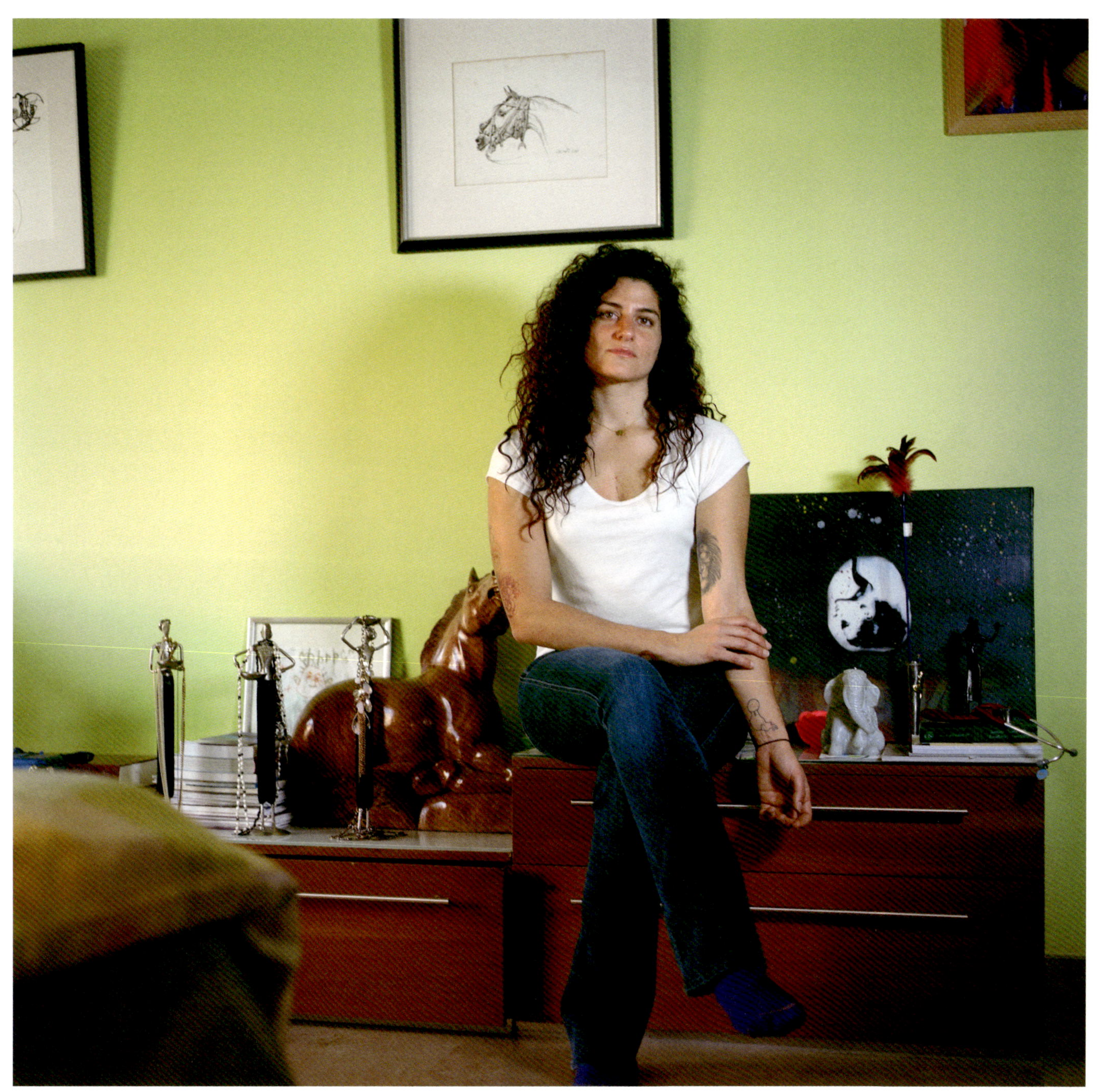

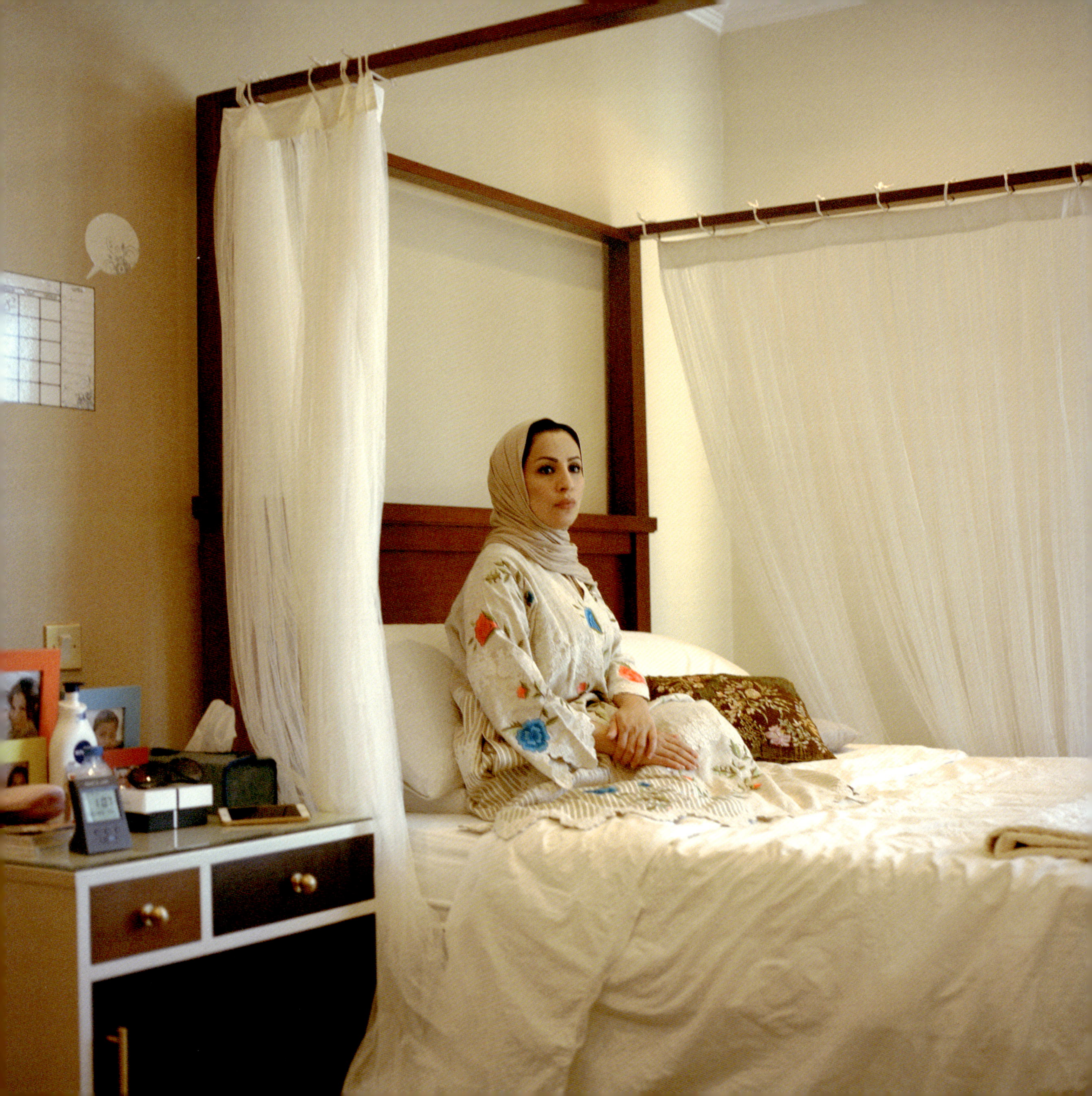

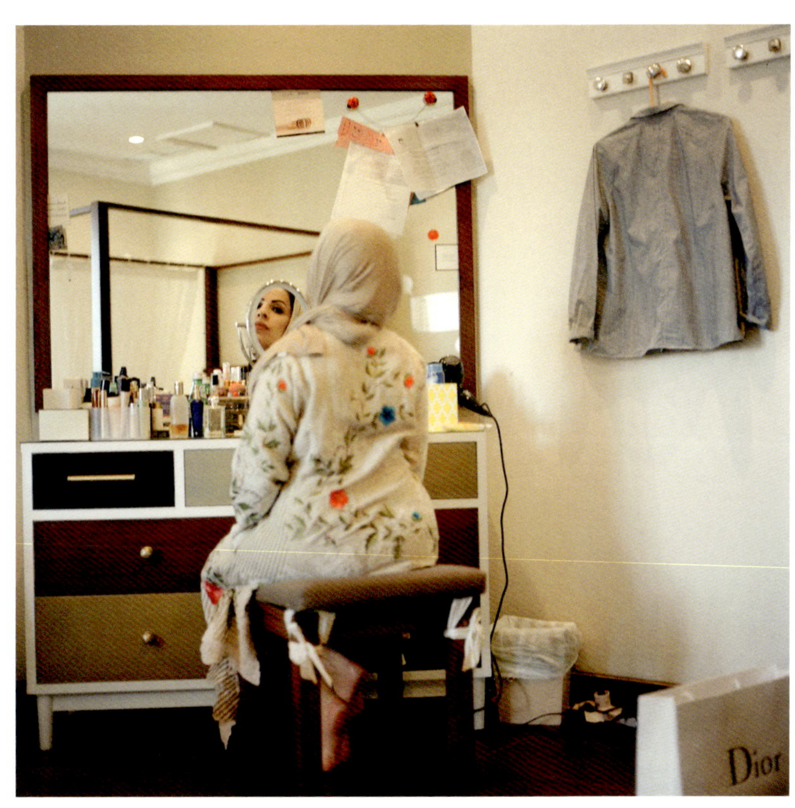
Dior

HANEEN AL-ASAKER

Daddy's Girl

Your mother knocks on your door at midnight. She is worried about your father, who went out for a late-night jog without his cell phone or wallet. You wait together until you receive the dreaded call. Your uncle arrives in person to break the news. The loss of your father unhinges your world. He was your rock. He held your hand on your first day at work. What does it mean to be yourself outside of his influence? You haven't any clue.

The fear of losing your loved ones persists despite the treatment you received. Now you treasure all the fleeting moments with your mother and son. Even when you are angry at one another, you cannot leave the house without her prayer. "Mama!" you beseech her, "bless me so I can return to you safe and sound." She will do it even when you drive her mad: "*Astawde-ik Allah allathy la tathee' wada-i-a-hu* (I leave you with the creator in whose protection nothing can be lost)."

You teach the blessing to your own son, who has seen the depth of your sadness. "Mama," he whispers when your chest is heavy with melancholy, "take my hand. I will give you my positive energy." You drive him to school every morning and play songs on the radio. More often than not, you will fight over your favorites. "Not fair!" he will shout playfully, "You played two Indian songs consecutively. I will choose the next two in a row." He prefers Western Top 40 to your Bollywood selection.

One day, you are so furious, you tell him to go to his room. You refuse to talk to him until he has learned his lesson. He does something else instead. From his own bedroom, he logs onto your television and plays your favorite Bollywood songs. Your body tingles all over. You fail to resist the music any longer and you call out his name. Your son rushes into your bedroom. He stands in formation. And you both perform the choreography. At night, before sleeping, you forget what you had been mad about.

RANA AL-OMANI

Privacy

You share a room with your older sister. On Fridays, you and your female sibling compete with your two brothers. Those with the cleaner room receive more allowance and, of course, bragging rights.

You settle in Boston to pursue an engineering degree. Your father helps you furnish your apartment. When he leaves, you hear it for the first time, your inner voice. You realize that you enjoy spending time alone. Up until now, however, you did not know the taste of solitude. In Kuwait, people view it as loneliness, so you are encouraged to seek the company of others, and this means, sometimes, enduring drama when it bursts onto the scene as moans and shrieks. Nobody told you that when you step away from the noise you will hear something else, at first soft and barely audible, internal signals that will guide the unfolding of your destiny.

Unlike your college friends who enjoy partying and clubbing on the weekends, you develop a tendency of staying at home. There you learn to cook for yourself. At first, you call your family to re-create the local dishes you would lick your fingers after eating. But as time goes on, you discover healthier options, fresher cuts, and farmers' markets. You agree with your inner voice. You feel a pull toward health and fitness, so when you return home, you leave your prestigious engineering degree among your Boston memorabilia in boxes, near flotsam and jetsam, untouched for fifteen years.

You find employment at a restaurant, baffling everyone. *A woman? With an engineering degree? From America? Cooking food for customers? Like an expat?* You never turn back. For you, baggage of the past fizzles away like steam on a burning pan. Yes, you have made friends in Boston for life, but your friendship is not built on history, or on future expectations. You stay grounded in the moment, building the present with determination, paying attention to the counsel of your inner voice. Labels and norms are needless garnish. In life, you choose dishes with less sugar and salt.

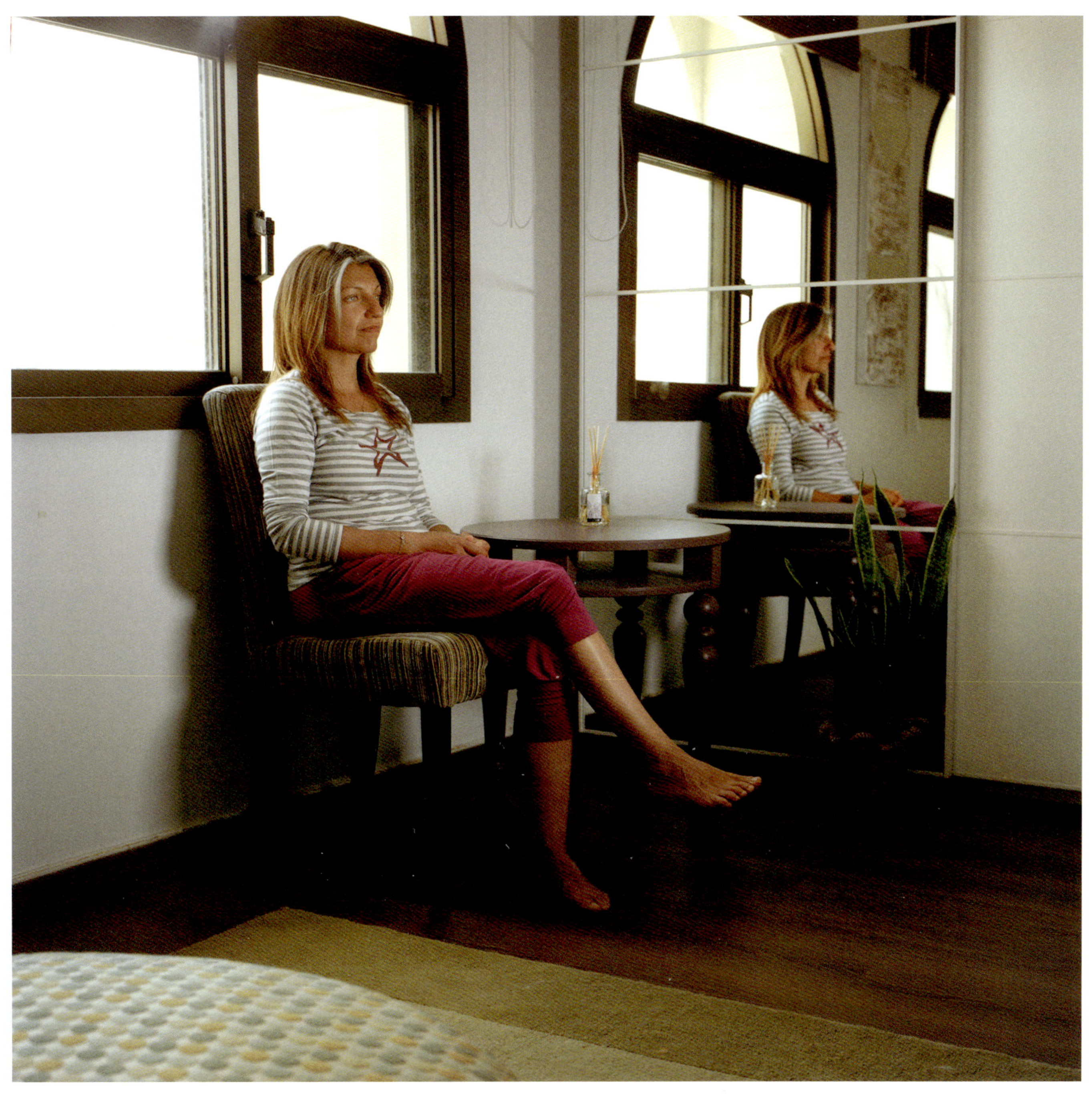

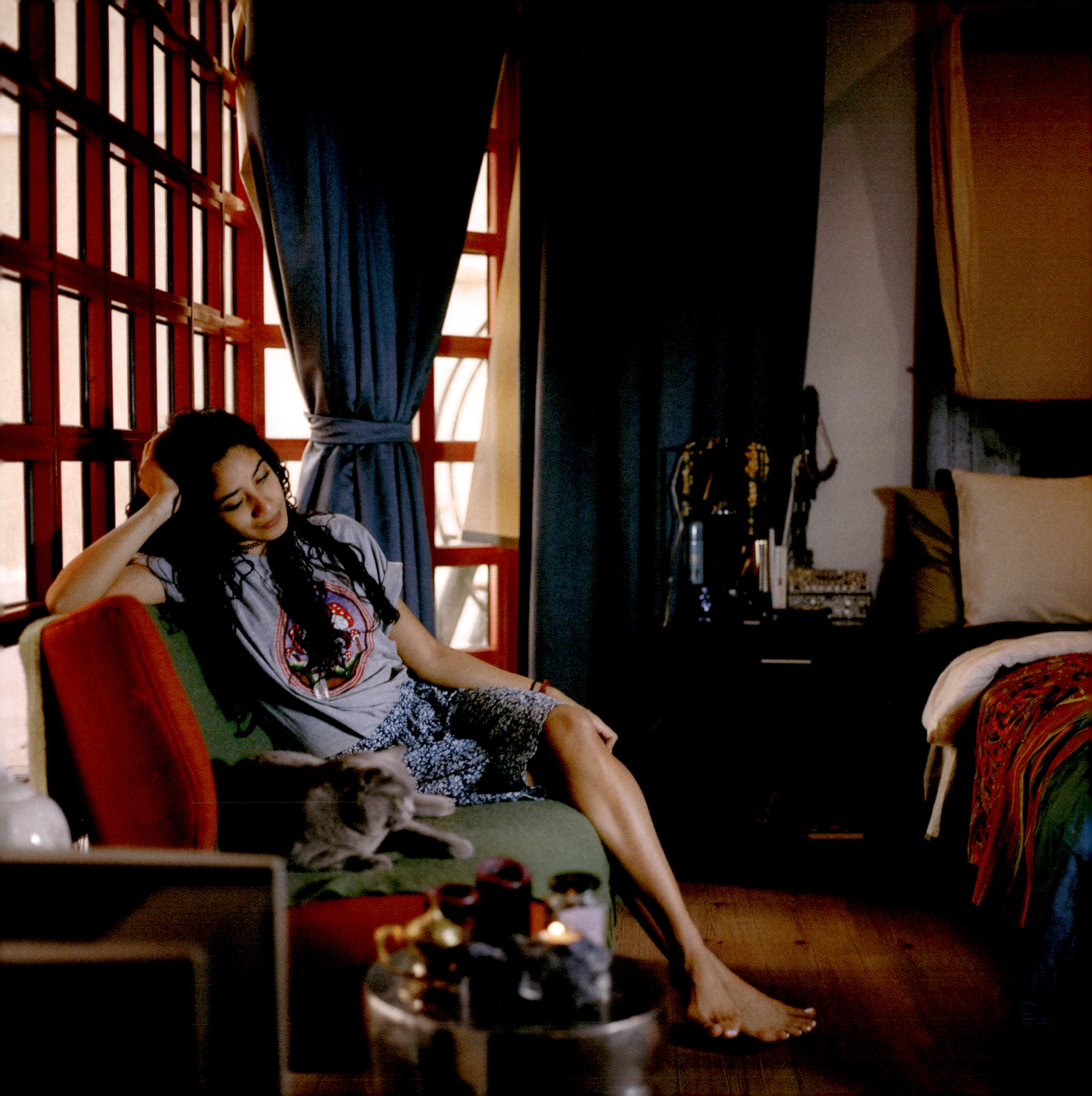

DALAL AL-MOHANNA

FLOW

You are two years old. In your mother's living room, guests gather around to cheer you on. You are wearing a tutu skirt and twirling with delight. Your mother reminds you constantly to be yourself.

You are on the street. It is nighttime. After your mother passes away, you are asked to vacate the house in which you have been living with your sisters. Hotels in Kuwait refuse you service. *Where are the husbands? The fathers? The adult brothers?* Because the eldest boy in the group is your seven-year-old nephew, you are a party of women and children, but the hotel staff disagree. Without a man, you cannot be a family.

On social media, you stumble on a girl hula-hooping. The circular band, spinning and whirling around her body, entices you to learn more about the sport. You buy one for yourself and struggle for days and weeks until, one night, you trip into the state of flow. The effect is so potent it helps you grieve the passing of your mother. You feel the presence of your body. You discover its contours, its passions. You bend the plastic expertly, you hang onto vibrations. You are now known as The Hula-Hoop Girl. In the Secret Garden, men and women dip into hoops and twirl, bypassing laws preventing dancing in public spaces.

Before furnishing your new apartment, you get a call from a magical being who tells you he is joining a circus. Can you come as well? Something deep within encourages you to forgo your reasoning for the moment, to connect instead to a deeper truth. Yes. You pack for a month. You arrive at the boat three days later. Your female captain walks a tightrope. You meet a trapeze couple swinging off the mast into each other's arms. A clown juggles next to your dancing magical friend. You practice your circus routines and bond together until the boat stops working in the middle of the ocean. You ride motorcycles around Indonesia teaching your circus craft to little boys and girls.

You run into a band of musical pirates who invite you onto their ship. You watch them raise their pirate flag. You feel the flutter of freedom rippling in your heart.

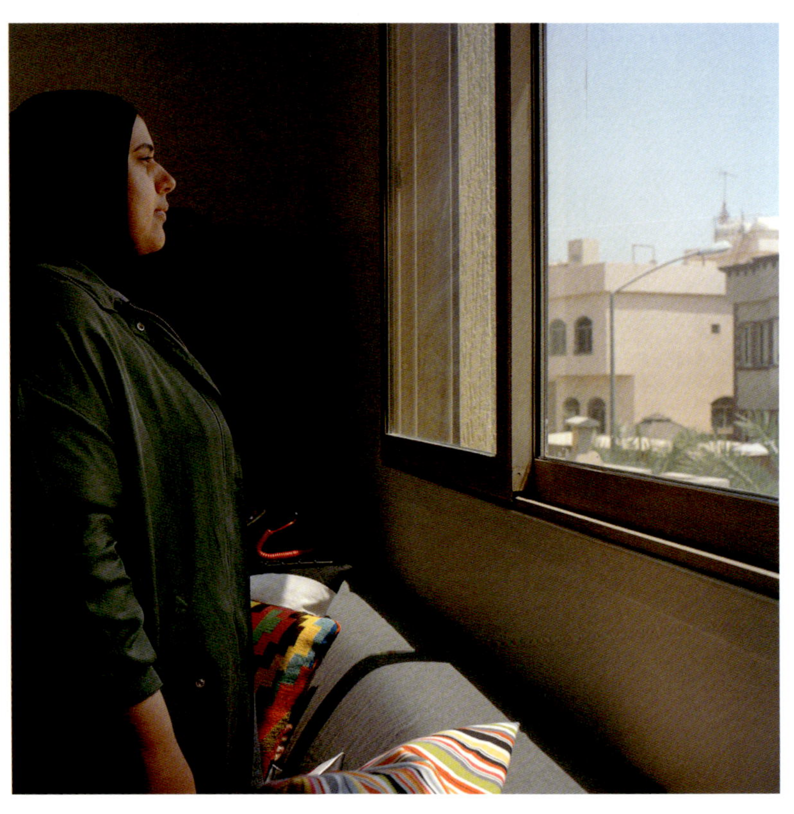

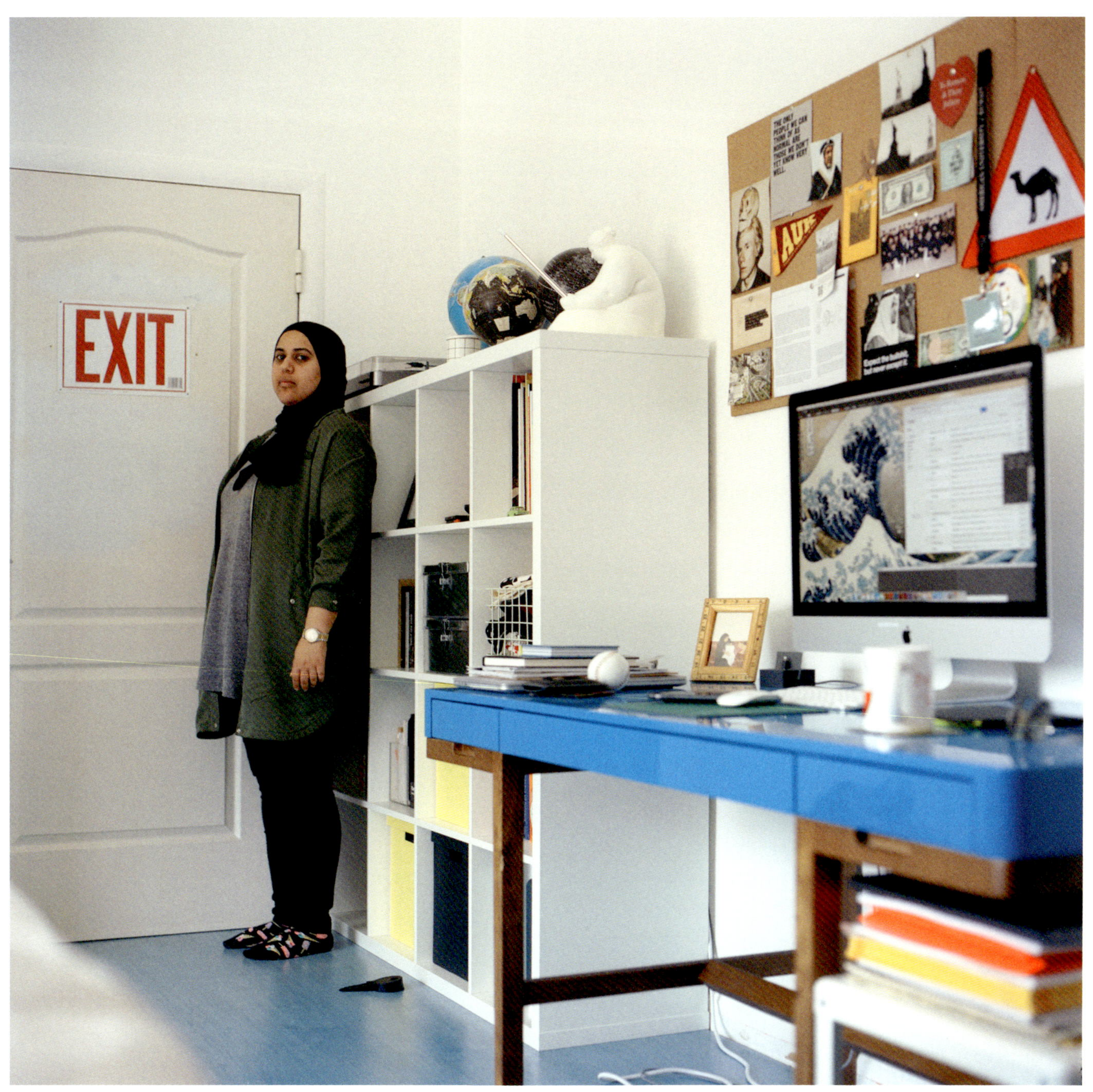
EXIT
THE ONLY PEOPLE WE CAN THINK OF AS NORMAL ARE THOSE WE DON'T YET KNOW VERY WELL.
AUK

MARIAM MANDANI

Unconditional Love

Your grandmother calls to congratulate you upon your enrollment at the American University of Kuwait. She hands the phone to your grandfather, who says, "You are now my colleague!"

"Do you know why he used that word specifically?" your grandmother asks when he returns the phone. "Your grandfather is an alum of the American University of Cairo, so you are his colleague."

You want to learn more. How did they get together? She tells you they met in Egypt when they were both university students. She had an operation. He visited the hospital daily with a bouquet of flowers, only managing to utter "Hello" before walking out the door. After her release from the hospital they became friends. That morphed into love, so he flew back home to ask her father for his approval. He returned to Egypt as her spouse.

You keep hearing your grandfather say he is heading downtown to work. You do not know it then but that is where you will conduct your business after graduating college as well. Whenever you take a picture in a city office and show it to family members, one of them tells you, "Did you know that Baba Wahab worked in the one across the street?"

Your family members notice the changes first. Your grandmother refuses to believe them until a visit to the doctor confirms their diagnosis. You pay attention and discover not only the forgetfulness, but a newfound openness. This man whom you have always admired, governor of the Central Bank, now sits on the couch next to you singing and laughing with more frequency. The first stage of Alzheimer's draws you closer. It feels short-lived. The intimacy is followed by more glaring acts of memory loss. He doesn't just forget the lyrics to the songs now, he even draws a blank when his own children enter the room. Then it is all gone. No more names are retained. No more shared experiences. Except for her: your grandmother. Baba Wahab still brightens whenever she walks into his room. And because you were named after her, he lights up when you are called too. This year, you gather with the other grandchildren to give Mama Mariam a framed photo of her younger self dancing with her sweetheart. You surprise her with a cake on which you have written: *Every love story is beautiful, but yours is our favorite.*

This elevated love deserves the wait and is worth every heartbreak until it is found. You refuse to surrender to social norms that would force you only to "settle down."

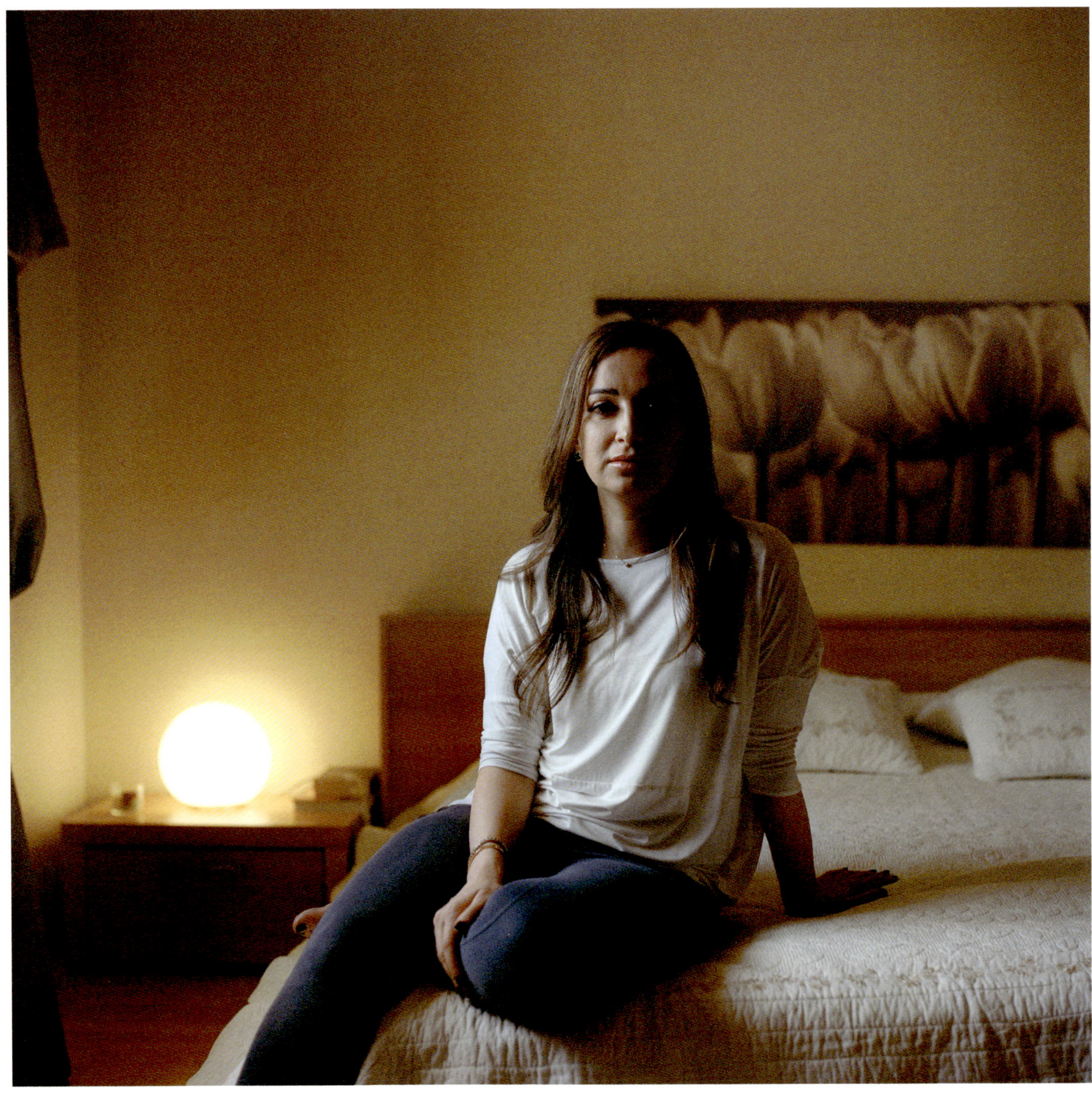

AISHA AL-SARRAJ

Language

Your Kuwaiti father met your Czechoslovakian mother on a road trip. He drove all the way from the Middle East to Europe. When he met your mother, they fell in love through letters written in the English language.

During the Invasion, your family travels to Switzerland where you add French to the three you already know. The story of communication does not stay in the realm of words. At the university, you study numbers. You work at the National Bank, where you meet your future husband. You fall in love with talking to one another. At night, even when the weather is hot, and despite the lack of suitable sidewalks, you still tie on your shoes and stroll through your neighborhood. You plan your travels together and set future goals and to-do lists.

Before sleeping, you check on your children, keeping the channels of communication open between all family members. You hear about their days and about their desires. You take your daughter to horseback-riding sessions, and you marvel at her perception when she tells you, "Mama, I think the brown horse is in love with the other one." You ask her why she thinks that. She tells you to pay attention to the way they look at each other. Hear the change in the tone of their whinnying call. And notice the gentleness with which they brush against each other's sides and necks and backs.

Your *babička* reminds you, "The more languages you learn, the more people you become." You are in the Czech Republic, in your grandmother's home, as young as your own daughter is now. Your gran's chicken is roasting in the oven. Your hands are full of warm eggs that you've just picked from the coop. Later in the day, you will stuff your hamster in your stroller and amble into the street alone. When you encounter strangers, they will laugh when they see your baby doll is in fact an animal.

You laugh now next to your daughter on the drive back home.

PHOEBE SALEM

Candle

You think you shine brightest in London. Though you are a junior architect, you are not designing toilet stalls like some of your friends. You are a master planner, erecting new cities in the Middle East. Your work takes you across the planet. You have been accustomed to looking down from the comfort of man-made steel. You meet people from all walks of life, royals and celebrities as well as earnest workers. Colombo comes to mind. At nights when you return to your apartment with fried food and chilled drinks, you say hi and mosey on to Whitechapel Street, where he would be sitting on the ground. You share your hot meal and cold drinks and talk about the world. One night when he asks for help getting up, you touch him for the first time and realize inside all that fabric puff is a small, frail man.

You have everything you ever wanted. Yet you continue to ache. The emptiness inside of you gapes larger the more you accomplish in your career. Without yoga, you might have stayed in London, but it helps you recognize the imbalance. The spark to travel in search of light and shadow is lit instantaneously. In a flat with a few close friends you host a going-away party. You braid your hair in seven knots and give each strand for a friend to cut.

The lessons you learn in India fan the flame of your desire. Years later when you return to your country, you choose to work for the government's master plan. And though it is near impossible to correct the mistakes of the past, you hope to at least start over, to build sustainable urban centers where candles light the wicks of souls. For as above, so below.

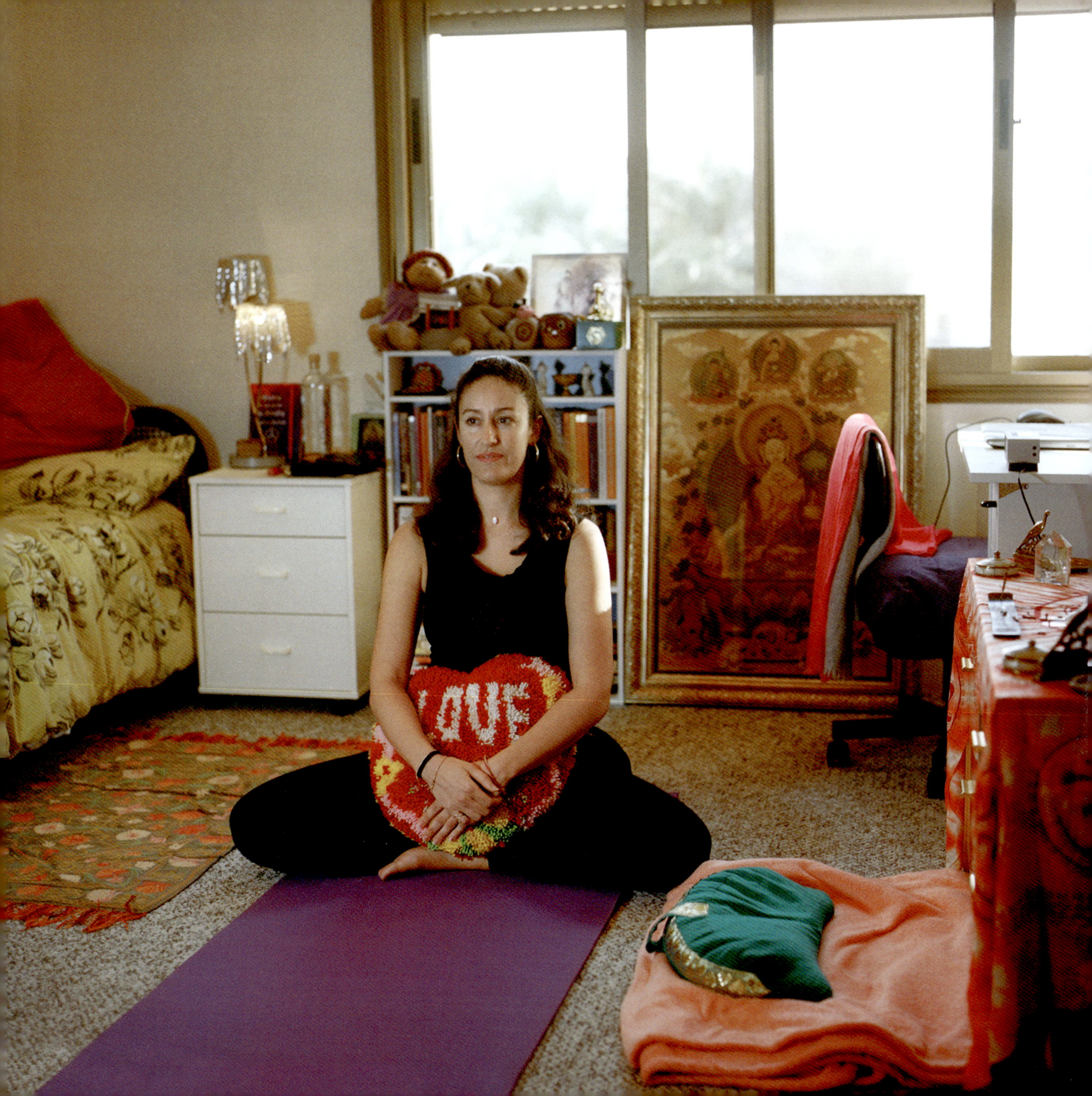
LOVE

XEINA AL-MUSALLAM

Leo

You work at a government agency. You don't lie to yourself about feeling superior; you do your work diligently, and that rubs co-workers the wrong way. One of them calls your name. She scrambles over only to inform you that you look sick. Too skinny to be healthy, and worse, your body lacks the curves Arab women are known for all over the world. You tell her, "At least I don't have cholesterol problems, and I'll live longer," then walk away.

You are born a ball of fire, and when you join Twitter in your mid-twenties, you discover how fervid your flames can get once your toes are stepped on by random men and women who cannot tell the difference between facts and opinions. You wish people would learn to extract their emotions from conversations, but it seems that nowadays most consider dialogues as war zones. So you pick your battles, because your energy is spent, and you intend to use your platform to counter misogynistic narratives by being the most authentic, unbridled version of yourself. In a world full of mainstream yea-sayers, you want to be an individual beacon of female confidence.

You cross your legs and the rim of your pencil skirt hikes up. Another colleague hurries over. She asks you, if a man were to seek your hand in holy matrimony on the condition that you start wearing more modest attire, how would you respond? You look her dead in the eyes and say, "I would never agree to marry someone that stupid, but thanks."

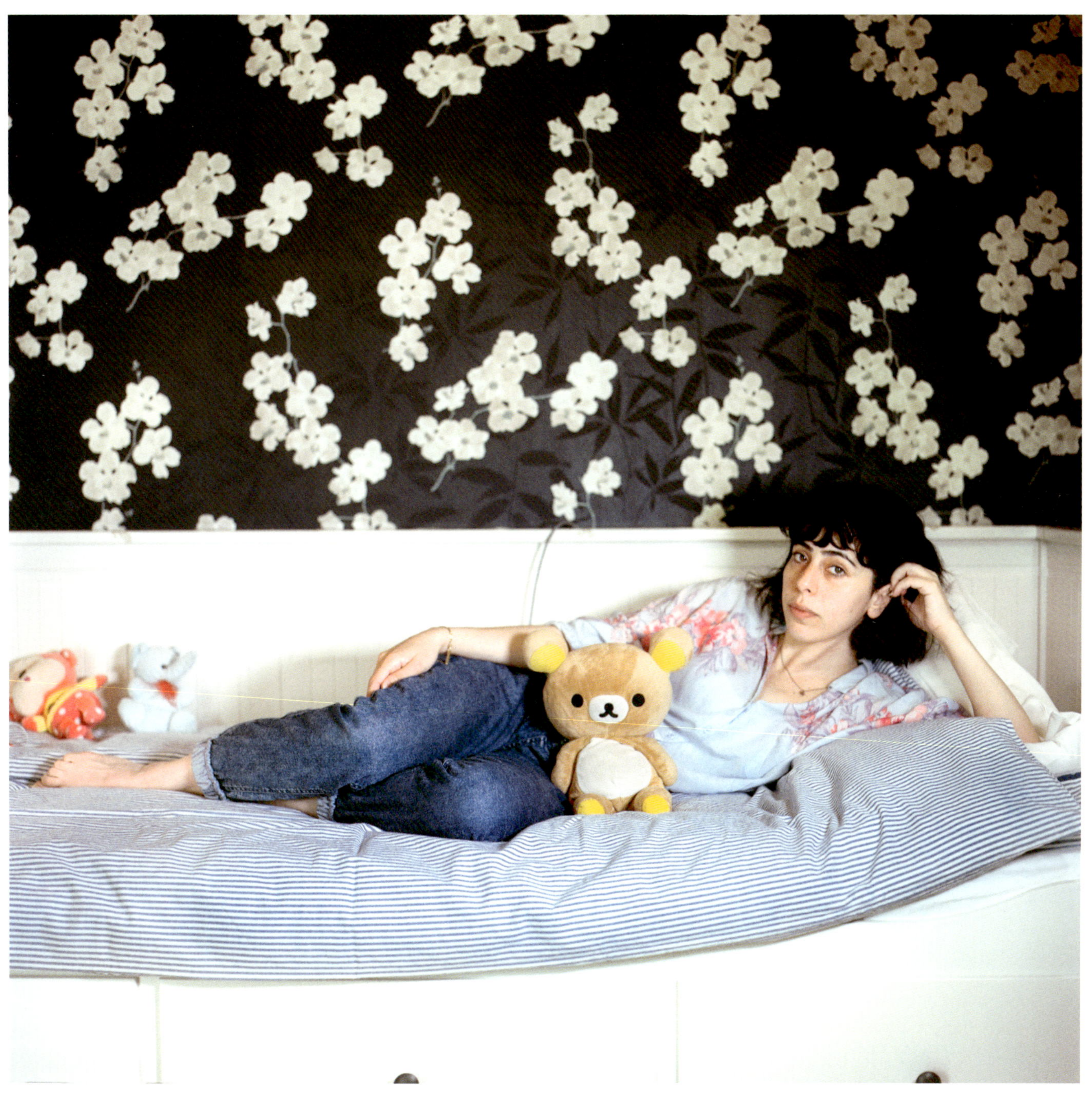

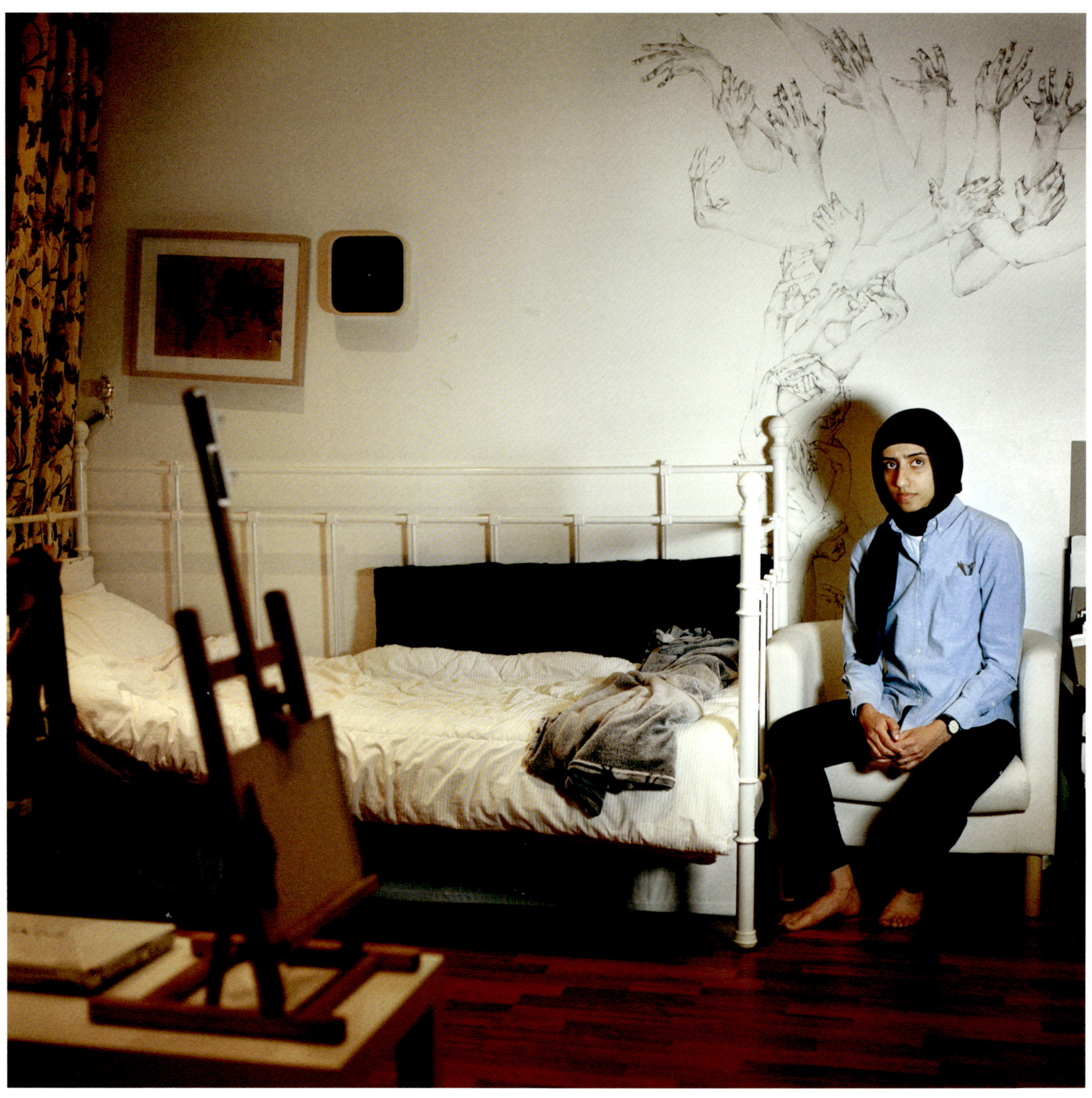

ZAHRA AL-MAHDI

In-Betweeness

In an open area in Rumaithiya—a *baraha*—in the late 1990s, you are surrounded by twenty prepubescent boys and girls, mostly cousins and relatives. You attach your digital contraption to your skateboard. It's one of your latest experiments. To motorize the wooden block on wheels you dismantle your personal computer and extract your modem, but the venture fails and a loud "Afaa!" echoes in the dusty afternoon air. It attracts the adults. Your father, who has always encouraged your flights of fancy and unconventional interests, takes you aside and says lovingly, "Some people might find the things you do, and the way you look while doing them, silly." You make silliness your modus operandi.

You are at Kuwait University, meeting people from different walks of life. Until then, you believed Kuwait comprised only conservative Shia. You befriend people on social media and visit a fancy gallery where you see Kuwaiti liberals for the first time. You realize after a while that they are not different from your religious aunts and uncles. The short dresses and popping colors are merely the other side of the coin of black abayas and veils pulled over chins. And you decide to relinquish the wide side of the coin to revel in the in-betweenness, not only sandwiched between conceptual extremes, but also amidst the geography of dirt and bricks and roads on the one hand, and that of virtuality, of effervescent potential, on the other. You dwell perpetually where being can flourish in many places at once.

ABEER AL-OMAR

Adventure

Your body is tied to five men. You are braving the icy wind, pulling together sledges containing food for the remainder of the trip, sleeping tents, and tools to deal with extreme weather and emergencies. When your team leader reaches the location where you will spend the night you all halt. After hours of constant trekking through the glacial plains you stop, not to take a break, but to construct a wall of ice, a protective shield from the frigid air so you can build, after that, your sleeping tents. The break only comes at night when you gather around a campsite fire to melt your cheese (your main source of protein) and sing songs and tell stories with the rest of your crew. You think to yourself, this is no different from the executive meetings. You used to be the only female participant in these events. The only female executive at the petrochemical company. But not anymore. Kuwait is changing, and you support the inclusivity. You think about the importance of teamwork, how it is cooperation, not competition, that ensures survival in the long term; how one slip or one accident can derail the entire expedition unless everyone unites their forces to provide support. You think about thinking itself, how losing focus means the difference between returning to the comfort of civilization and never waking again, so you stay in the present; any baggage, any fear of upcoming events, any butterflies in one's stomach, need to be quelled without mercy. Once the strategy is developed, once the terrain is mapped, once the goals and the resources are analyzed and the roles distributed, there is no more chance for weakness or second-guessing. You plunge into the challenge with all your might. The testing comes naturally to you because your hunger is not for accolades or adoration but for growth. You love the adventure because it changes you, because it builds you from the inside out. You love the danger that comes with climbing mountains and weathering stormy seas, because you are a human in competition with only Abeer, and you will always bet on the present version to vanquish the you of yesterday.

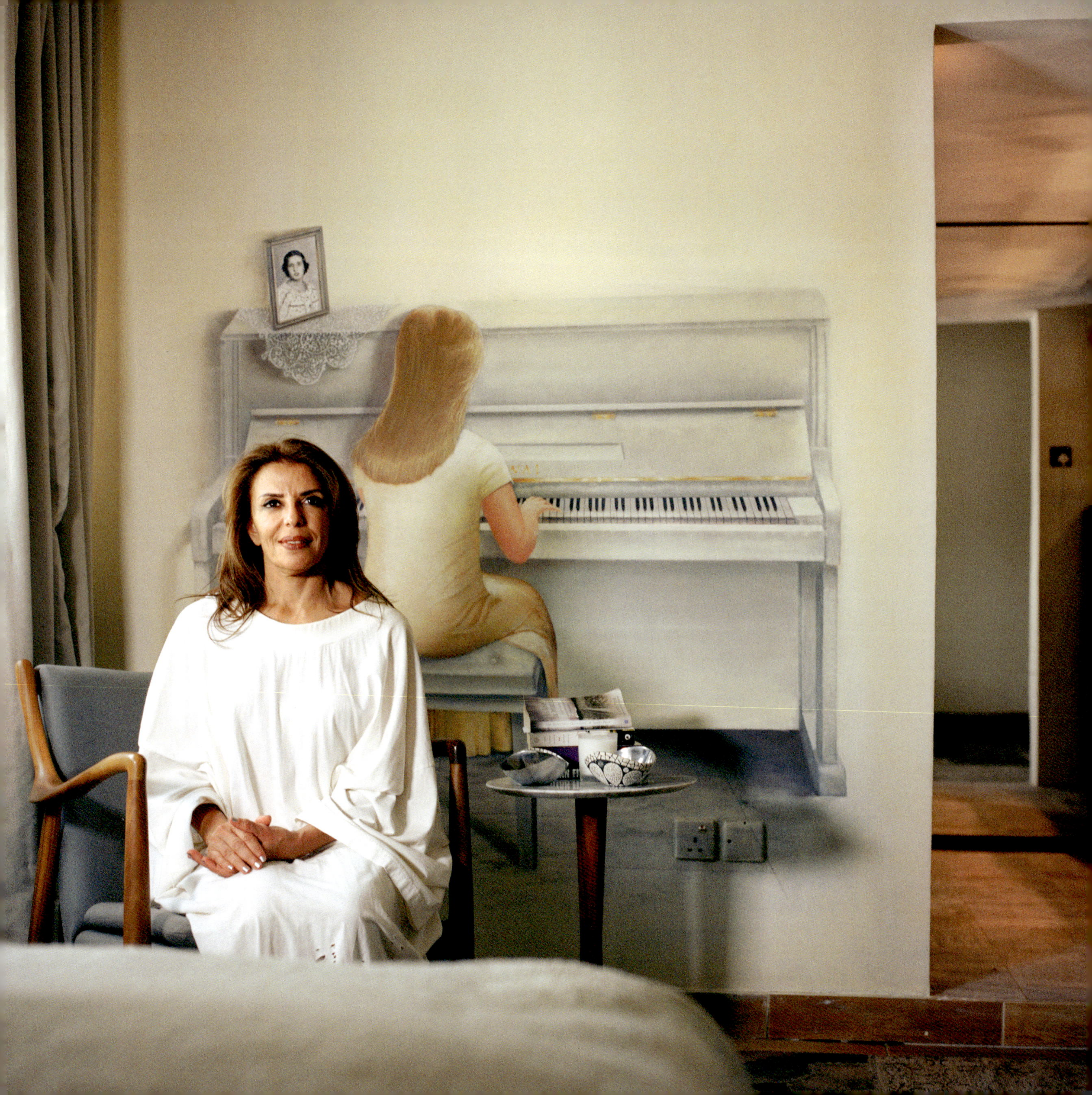

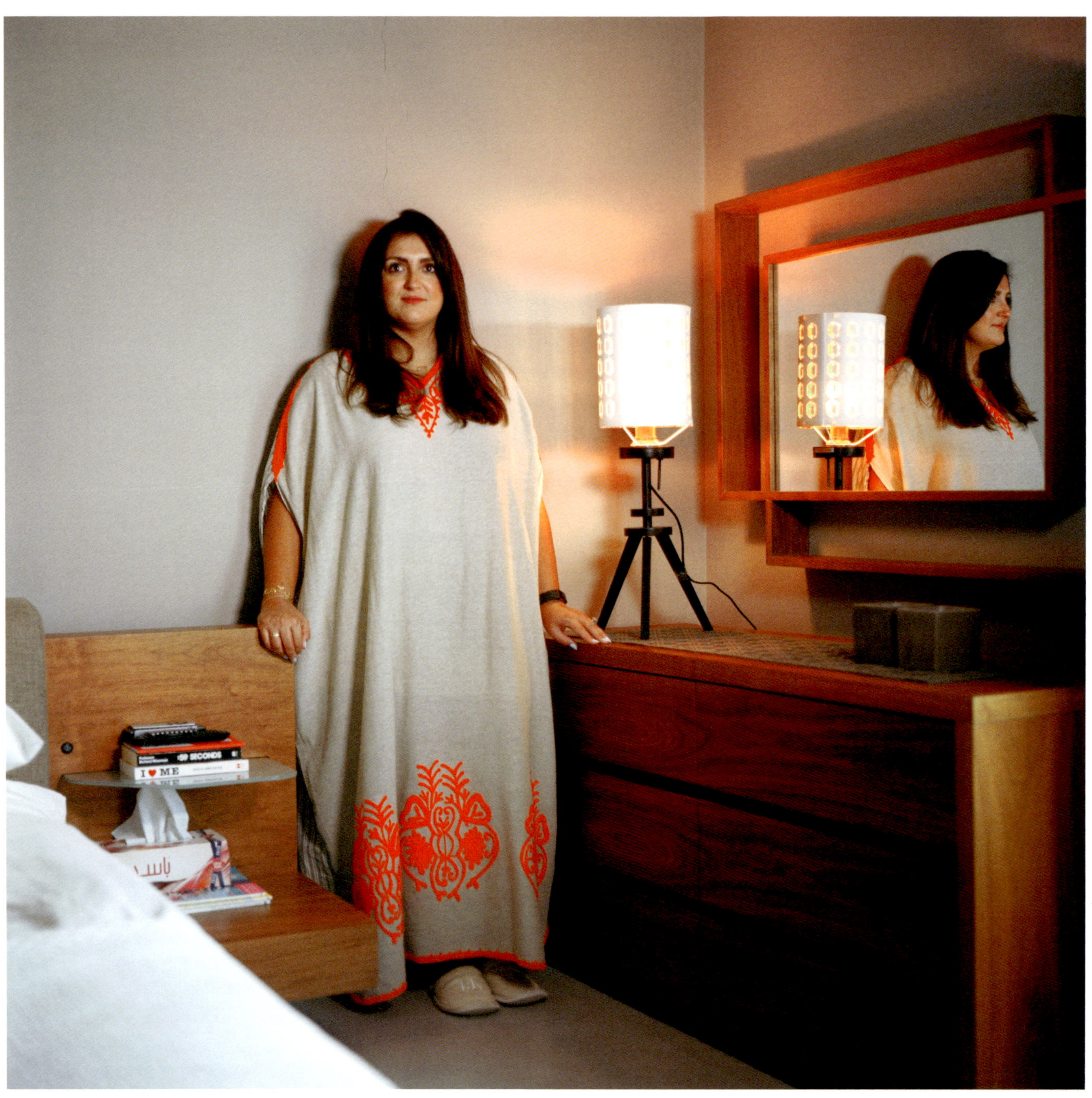
SECONDS
I ♥ ME

RASHA AL-DOUGACHI

Ringtons Tea

You wake up at 5:30 a.m. on the dot. You shower like clockwork. You don appropriate attire and march on toward the breakfast table where you slather warm toast with jam and butter, and sip Ringtons tea. The rest of the day unfolds with comfortable predictability. You drive to the British School of Kuwait. You attend a staff briefing. You impart today's lessons before joining other teachers in the staff room, where you exchange everything from expertise to entertaining stories about the locals, as though you were not one of them yourself, being half Kuwaiti and half British.

You want to wake up at nine, or ten, or—for crying out loud—eleven! But your body is so heavy. Your eyelids refuse to part. Your anxiety is weighing you down, shackling you to the mattress, and the bed to the ground. You can barely crawl your way into the shower, barely stumble down the staircase to the breakfast table. The Ringtons tea is still there, but now it is accompanied with sweets, so many of them you cannot fit into your appropriate attire anymore. And yet you cannot do without them, they give you the boost necessary to handle another debacle at the ministry. How many more days can get wasted because employees bark orders—"*Hnak!*" or "*Hnee!*"—but they won't tell you where "there" or "here" is. The people beside them ignore your pleading eyes. They scoff at any interruptions. They point at nowhere and everywhere, waving two or three fingers like hurricanes, "Not here! Not here!" The only thing clear to you is that they want you out of their sight, and they can yell you out of their vicinity if you linger. So it takes days, weeks, and then months, to finalize requirements for your new venture. It is difficult to muster motivation when you park in front of the ministry building. You know you wanted this. You left the comfort of schedules and briefings and colleagues sharing information on how to become an entrepreneur, a businesswoman, and launch your own bakery. But the bureaucratic hell is unbearable and so you spend an hour crying in your car. Every day you wonder how much more tears are left inside of you before you shrivel up.

Now you wake up at 5:45 a.m. on the dot. You leap out of bed and skip to your breakfast table to enjoy your Ringtons tea (without the jam and butter, or even the sweets). You share a hearty conversation with your family members, then drop your daughters at school. From there it's straight to the gym where you pump up your heart rate on the treadmill and hop from one machine to the next. The early dopamine hit, you have learned, is crucial to raising one's mood. Thanks to the life coach you hired because you wanted to be empowered like the locals who seem to handle the ministry visits and business requirements with confidence, your world transformed. You told the life coach you were tired of timidity, tired of anxious thoughts imprisoning your potential. Once you made that mental switch you realized that the biggest hindrance to the business wasn't the discourteous officials, or the sudden influx of violations that pop out of nowhere, not the lack of a fraternal infrastructure where business owners share their lessons, or your own genetics and upbringing, that sense of Britishness that conflicted with Kuwaiti fervor. Rather, it was your worldview itself. Once you reworked your expectations you uncovered a treasure trove of courage. You learned to be practical and independent. You found comfort in the messiness of a day sans schedules and briefings, because, from an entrepreneurial point of view, it meant untapped potential. You bring this new worldview to your business.

NOHA AL-MANSOUR

Big Fish

All your life, you think people are inherently good. You languish on a cushion with loving parents. You dance in front of the late Amir on stage before Iraq invades Kuwait. "*Mino Ile Yahmiha* (Who will protect her?)," you sing to the crowd. You only realize the extent of the bubble when you embark on your first business deal. Your partner swindles you out of your capital, and you struggle to pay your debt. In that moment, you learn two lessons.

One, we live in a Big Fish Eat Little Fish world; this business about people being inherently good is a myth. You refuse to teach it to your own children. You never want to see them decompose in the bellies of sharks. If you are not the biggest in the room, then you're a catch. There is no right or wrong about this philosophy. It's just a fact.

Two, failure is the first step to conquest. Though you scarmble to pay your debt back you realize that the business venture gave you monumental exposure. You use that visibility to brand yourself. Your work gains the attention of the Amir, and you are asked to design the customs for National Day. So you tell your children: "Always fail. Never hold back for fear of shame or even pain. The more you fail, the fewer doors will lock in your future—in fact, the opposite of closure will take place. The opportunities you create through failure tend to clear the stream toward uncontestable achievements if you remain steadfast and focused. So make fools of yourselves. Get hurt. Lose, and lose again. But do not stray from your current, or else you attract the whales. And none can help you then."

Your teenage son tells you he wants to dive. For all your indoctrination, you still cry, out of fear that he might hurt himself. It is he who reminds you of your belief system. "Don't you always say, fail and make mistakes?" You nod, your face still wet. "Then let me dive, Mama. I am hungry for success."

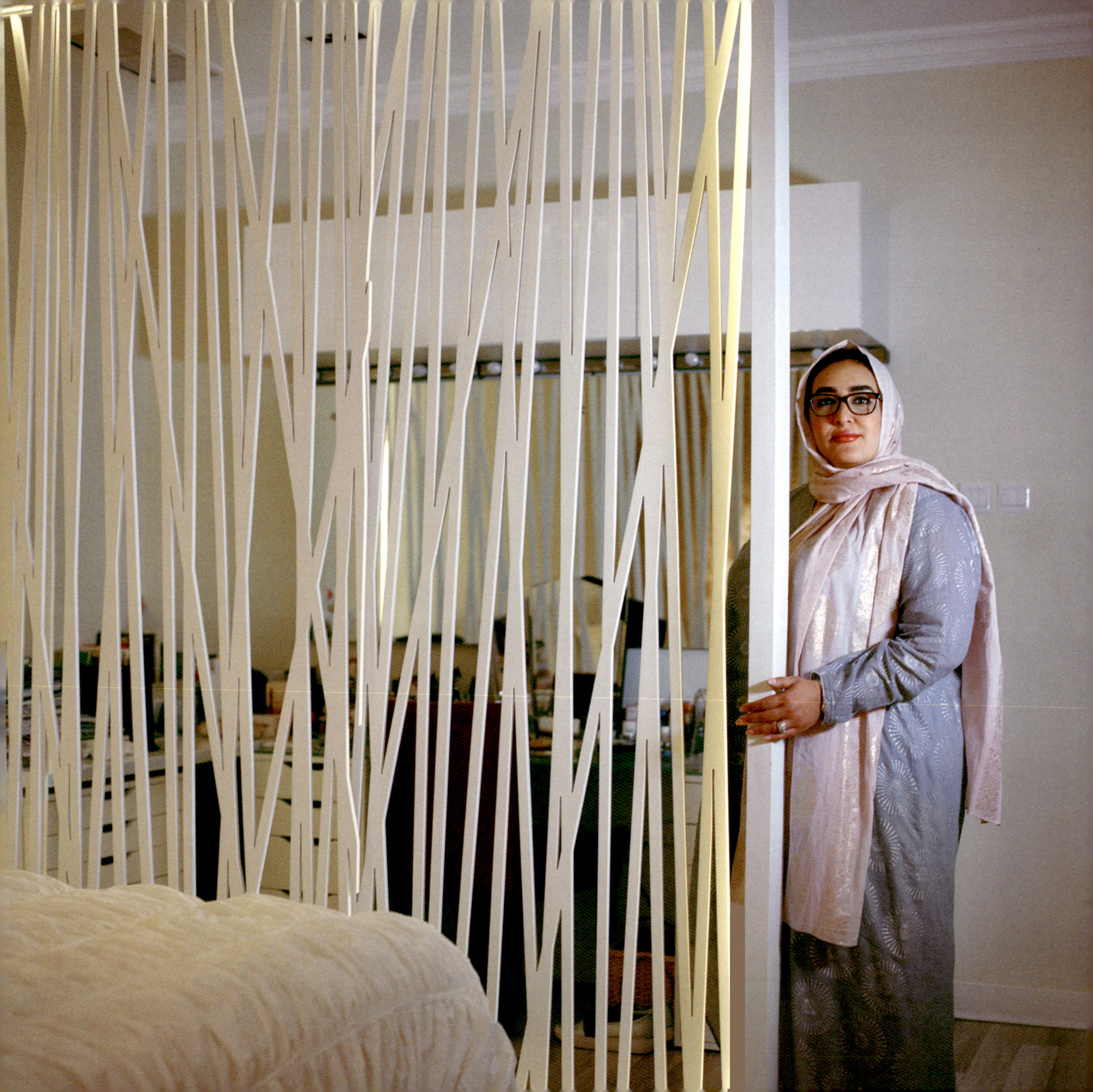

ACKNOWLEDGMENTS

First and foremost, I wish to thank Mama Fozia for her support of this publication on women of Kuwait. Her contribution to my crowdfunding was extremely generous. This book would never have seen the light of day without you.

A very special thank-you to my beloved mother, Shaikah. You always believed in my dreams, even if you didn't always like them. Thank you for the love, and your endless support.

A special thank-you to my siblings, Haneen, Suliman, and Hamad, for supporting this project. With all of our differences, we always love and support each other.

I am deeply grateful to Blink for supporting this project. I am lucky to be part of the Blink family.

This project would not have been possible without the backing of many supporters who saw the potential in this book, including:

Alanoud Alsabah, Hussa Al Humaidhi, Grace Diamond, Abeer Alomar, Matt Borowick, Dalal Aldoub, Rana Aomani, Sarah bn Shukr, Rafael Tiago Flores da Cunha, Sebastien Vergne, Anas Amoudi, Samaher Bayazeed, Saif Alharthi, Eman AlBedah, Awatif Salman Alsabah, Francesca Ferrero, Māra Zoltners, Taibah Alahmad, Zahra AlMousa, Javier Sirvent, Hiyam Alfassam, Sam Bodenstein, Hala Almughni, Mai Al Moataz, Frank Iannazzo-Simmons, Aseel Al Yaqoub, Rick Schatzberg, David Mager, Marzia Gamba, Awatef Alessa, Thom Sanchez, Khalifa Alrashed, Fahad Alostad, Florence Nasar, Joyce, Bassam Shuhaibar, Alina Zolotareva, Catherine Night, Reem Alomani, Farah Khajah, Maha Alotaibi, Sharifa Alsuleity, Amnah Almutawa, Alex Fisz-bein, Maggie Svoboda, Terri F. Hodara, Khaled Alkhashram, Beyoona Dashti, Mohammad Dashti, Michael Challita, Hawraa Maqseed, Laredo Montoneri, Abrar Alebrahim, Camilla Cerea, Jude Anasta, Matt Low, Abigail Simon, Fatma Makki, Mugren Ohaly, Marc Mcandrews, Mohamed Somji, Dalal Almohanna, Naief Alahmad, Nadira Husain, Max Aggrey, Barbara

Giacoman, Jawaher M., Pilar Torcal Moreno, Sulaiman Al-Salahi, PhotoShelter, Susan Grant, Krisanne Johnson, Monica Shie, Dan Ragan, Mona Almazidi, Raphael Shammaa, Lindsay Herr, Roni Goren Ben-Zvi, Haitham Alkanderi, Federico Cruz, Iris Wu, Jean Christian Jung, Janet Miller, Fawzia, Arkadiy Stepanchuk, Ilona Ru, Amanda Doueihi, Ella Joy Meir, Melanie Landsm, Mark Balahadia, Didem Civginoglu, Cate Dingley, Lucia Buricelli, Meredith Edwards, Kerstin Costa & Francois Chevresson, Fahed Al-Sumait, Nasrah Omar, Ben Berlin, Samyukta Lakshmi, Mo Scarpelli.

To the 25 women who have shared their stories and space with me: I will always be grateful for you.

Thank you to Nada Faris, who collaborated with me in this book. Thank you for believing in my project, and for the time and energy you invested in every woman in this book. You made it easy for each one to open up to you and to share their stories with the world. Thank you for being Nada.

Jassim Alnasrallah, thank you for your beautiful calligraphy. Thanks to your contribution, we have a magnificent cover.

Thank you to Ursula Damm for conveying the heart and soul of the project through your design. Thank you for your patience and your amazing communication. You have helped me in this journey to create my first book.

Thank you to my friends, especially Marzia Gamba: you believed in me.